Urban Migration and
Economic Development in Chile

M.I.T. MONOGRAPHS IN ECONOMICS

Urban Migration and Economic Development in Chile

BRUCE H. HERRICK

THE M.I.T. PRESS

Massachusetts Institute of Technology
Cambridge, Massachusetts, and London, England

Acknowledgments

This book, originally conceived as a doctoral dissertation for the Department of Economics at the Massachusetts Institute of Technology, is the product of intellectual stimulation and cooperation from a number of sources. My thesis advisors, M.I.T. Professors Charles Myers, Evsey Domar, and Abraham Siegel, were instrumental in shaping my thinking about the problems to which the book addresses itself. In Santiago, Carlos Massad, then Director of the University of Chile's Institute of Economics, placed the resources of the Institute at my disposal. Almost every investigator on the Institute's staff responded to my questions at one time or another. In addition, at the Latin American Center for Demography in Santiago, Carmen Miró and Juan Elizaga graciously extended some of their unpublished data and the use of their tabulation equipment.

At the University of California, Los Angeles, Miss Pat Mays brought an uncommonly large fund of stenographic patience and good humor to bear on the manuscript.

Finally, the entire study was done with the financial assistance of the Foreign Area Fellowship Program (formerly the Ford Foundation Foreign Area Training Fellowship Program). As should be clear, however, the conclusions, opinions, and other statements in this book are mine and not necessarily those of the Fellowship Program nor of any of the people whose help is hereby gratefully acknowledged.

Los Angeles, California   Bruce Herrick
September 1965

v

Contents

Tables

ix

Urban Migration and
Economic Development in Chile

1

Introduction

Many problems face the nation trying to extricate itself from a position of low income. Prescriptions for the cure of these problems come from many sources; some of these prescriptions are meaningless, others contradictory. The underdeveloped country is told that it must concentrate on physical capital formation, but that investment in human beings is also important. It must stimulate savings at the same time that it improves basic living standards. General education is to be stressed, but technically trained manpower is a *sine qua non* for development. Industrialization should be emphasized, but not at the expense of agricultural production and productivity nor in disregard of the laws of international comparative advantage.

Each of these choices is difficult, but in one way or another the underdeveloped country will have to make all of them, implicitly by inaction, if not explicitly by positively stated goals and attempts at movement toward these goals. Over-all, given higher productivity in the industrial sector than in other economic activities catering to domestic demand, we might be tempted to agree with Professor Ranis that "the criterion of 'success' in the development effort may be stated as a rate of industrial labor absorption in excess of the rate of population growth."[1] Elsewhere he states that "the heart of the development problem lies in the gradual shifting of the economy's center of gravity from the agricultural to the industrial sector through labor reallocation."[2] Clearly these events can occur only

[1] Gustav Ranis, "Allocation Criteria and Population Growth," *American Economic Review*, Vol. 53, No. 2 (May 1963), 623.
[2] John C. H. Fei and Gustav Ranis, "Innovation, Capital Accumulation, and Economic Development," *American Economic Review*, Vol. 53, No. 3 (June 1963), 283. By the same authors, see also "A Theory of Economic Develop-

when a sufficiently large fraction of the labor force moves physically from traditional to more modern activities.

At the same time, we would not expect to see urban migration and economic stagnation occurring together. Urban migration is usually considered as a series of events occurring in a dynamically changing economy. In the absence of any movement, when rural fertility exceeds urban fertility (expressed as number of live births per thousand of population), the agricultural labor force will grow faster than industrial employment. Movement from the countryside to the towns, necessary if strictly balanced growth of the two parts of the labor force is to occur, becomes even more imperative if an increase in the size of the industrial sector is among the goals of the developing economy. This response of labor to a changing industrial structure and to its increasing demands for factors of production is usually viewed cheerfully as evidence of a society's dynamism and economic flexibility.

We can, however, suggest a model in which the urban migration is not such a clear sign of well-being in the economy. The value of a worker's output in agriculture, instead of improving over time, may actually stagnate or decline as a result of outmoded land tenure arrangements, excessive division of land parcels, backwardness of the cultivators, unfavorable terms of trade, or other disincentive factors. Rural poverty may thus force young laborers, the children of farm families, into the cities to look for work. These migrants, sometimes lacking in education or occupational skills, may only be able to drift into tiny handicraft shops, unskilled work in construction, or personal services, rather than find employment in a growing modern industrial sector.

Thus the usual signs of economic development — urban migration accompanied by expanding secondary and tertiary sectors and relatively contracting primary ones — are seen. But development, here thought of as "industrialization" — the growth within the economy of technologically advanced, high-productivity activities — is not occurring. Failure of incomes to grow may be only one manifestation of this frustrated shift in the industrial distribution of the labor force without corresponding economic growth. Signs such as political unrest and an increase in demagogic appeals by public and

ment," *American Economic Review*, Vol. 51, No. 4 (September 1961), 533–565. These articles appear, substantially unaltered, as chapters in their book, *Development of the Labor Surplus Economy* (Homewood, Illinois: Richard D. Irwin, 1964).

would-be public figures may also accompany the stagnation. The vociferous demands for social services by the new urban agglomerations will bump against the country's financial ability to provide these services, since increases in governmental spending power may be hampered by the failure of the economy to place the new workers in more productive occupations.

The Chilean economy during the period from 1940 to 1960 provides an interesting example of a country in which incipient tendencies toward economic development decayed into stagnation and in which urban migration assumed a form reflecting the economic and demographic conditions surrounding it. This book tries to coordinate the record of Chile's economic development with an account of its concomitant internal migration. In particular, shifts in urban population and changes in the structure of the labor force are explored in an attempt to understand migration's role in economic development.

Economic Background[3]

Chile falls mid-range in the spectrum of underdeveloped countries. It is neither among the least developed, as are those African and Asian nations with per capita incomes of less than $100 per year, nor is it among the most developed of the underdeveloped countries, as is Argentina with its per capita income of $700–$800.

Instead Chile is one of those countries whose per capita annual income of $300–$400 means that many of its citizens can live without worrying every day about the most pressing needs of subsistence. On the other hand, the strength of the people's desire for further development can easily be visualized. Movies and magazines remind them constantly that the United States has a much higher average income, estimated at from five to eight times the Chilean figure. Of course, the styles of life portrayed by these mass media may exaggerate in the minds of the Chileans the differences between their country and the more developed ones. This exaggeration in turn creates aspirations which, in the absence of development, are frustrated by the lack of economic progress.

[3] The most useful sources of background data and their interpretation for the Chilean economy are two publications of the Institute of Economics of the University of Chile: *Desarrollo económico de Chile 1940–1956* (Santiago, 1956) and *La economía de Chile en el período 1950–1963* (Santiago, 1963); hereafter cited as *Desarrollo económico* and *La economía de Chile,* respectively.

The central fact in recent Chilean economic history was the deterioration in the annual rate of growth of per capita incomes from 1.5% in the decade of the 1940's to 0.3% in the 1950's.[4] Choosing different periods provides an even darker picture: income per capita rose by 1.9% per year between 1940 and 1952, while in the subsequent period 1952–1960 it actually declined by 0.5% per year.

This flaccid economic behavior contrasts strongly with the expectations derived from the enthusiastic writings of some Chilean observers. They point to the agricultural and mineral resources, the intelligence and education of the labor force, and the comparative efficiency of the civil service.[5] These advantages, viewed in the abstract, make growth seem almost unavoidable. Even discounting these praises suitably, the impression remains that the capability for economic development is present. But inflation, the nature of the income distribution, and agricultural and industrial developments all played their parts in depressing the rate of growth during the 1950's.

Chileans have endured inflation for more than eighty years. Its long life has been coupled with a virulence which in other countries led to hyper-inflation. Chile, however, has always become sufficiently alarmed to take corrective steps when runaway inflation threatened.[6] When price rises of less than 20% per year during the 1940's ballooned into increases of more than 60% per year on the average between 1953 and 1956, price stabilization finally became a political imperative. The stabilization program resulted in reducing

[4] Corporación de Fomento de la Producción, *Cuentas nacionales de Chile 1940–1962* (*cifras provisionales revisadas*); (Santiago, 1963; mimeographed), p. 42. Hereafter cited as *National Accounts*. Measurements of long-term gains in production are contained in Marto Ballesteros and Tom E. Davis, "Growth of Output and Employment in Basic Sectors of the Chilean Economy," *Economic Development and Cultural Change*, Vol. 11, No. 2, Part 1 (January 1963), 152–176.

[5] A good example of an appraisal of these resources is Merwin L. Bohan and Morton Pomeranz, *Investment in Chile — Basic Information for U.S. Businessmen* (Washington, D. C.: U.S. Department of Commerce, 1960), pp. 6–8.

[6] The causes and effects of the inflation are tangential to this work and are ably described by others. See Albert Hirschman, *Journeys Toward Progress* (New York: Twentieth Century Fund, 1963), Chapter 3; Joseph Grunwald, "The 'Structuralist' School on Price Stability and Development: The Chilean Case" in Albert Hirschman (ed.), *Latin American Issues* (New York: Twentieth Century Fund, 1961), pp. 95–123; and Arnold C. Harberger, "The Dynamics of Inflation in Chile," in Carl F. Christ *et al.*, *Measurement in Economics — Studies in Mathematical Economics and Econometrics* (Stanford, Calif.: Stanford University Press, 1963), pp. 219–250.

the rate of inflation to a relatively mild 25% per year from 1956 to 1960.

Inflation depressed saving and investment. The shrinkage in the real value of money discouraged conventional saving while the uncertainties inherent in the variable speed of the inflation made investment more risky than it would have been under a more predictable inflation. Table 1.1 compares the weakness in Chile's gross

TABLE 1.1

GROSS DOMESTIC FIXED CAPITAL FORMATION AS A PERCENTAGE OF GROSS DOMESTIC PRODUCT: CHILE AND OTHER LATIN AMERICAN COUNTRIES

Country	Period	GDFCF/GDP
Chile	1950	9.0%
	1951	9.5
	1952	9.3
	1953	9.1
	1954	8.0
	1955	8.3
	1956	8.3
	1957	10.7
	1958	10.5
	1959	9.7
	1960	10.6
	1961	13.3
	1962	12.4
Brazil	1954–1956	14.7
	1957–1959	14.4
Mexico*	1954–1956	14.6
	1958–1960	15.2
Argentina*	1954–1956	20.9
	1958–1960	23.1
Peru	1954–1956	23.5
	1957–1959	21.6

* Gross domestic fixed capital formation as a percentage of gross national (instead of domestic) product.

Sources: United Nations, National Accounts Yearbook 1961 (New York, 1962); Corporación de Fomento, National Accounts, op. cit., pp. 8, 10.

domestic fixed capital formation as a percentage of gross domestic product with that of other Latin American countries in the 1950's.[7]

[7] These other countries increased their gross national product per capita from four and one-half to fifteen times as fast as Chile. Using data from the United Nations' Yearbook of National Accounts Statistics and Demographic Yearbook and the International Monetary Fund's International Financial Sta-

The sources of this capital formation are also revealing.[8] Between 1950 and 1962, private saving was positive only in 1950, 1953, and 1956. Coincidentally, 1956 was the year that President Ibáñez and the Klein-Saks mission, frightened at the severity of the inflation during the immediately preceding years, began their heavily publicized stabilization effort.[9] Even the addition of government saving sufficed to make total *net* saving positive in only six of the thirteen years 1950–1962. The remainder, and indeed the bulk, of the financing of gross domestic capital formation came from provisions for fixed capital consumption — mostly from depreciation reserves.

Conditions in agriculture also contributed to sluggish Chilean development. Once again the decade of the 1950's showed substantially different characteristics than the 1940's. As Table 1.2 shows, production per worker and income generated per worker in agriculture both rose by 1.8% annually during the 1940's. Although physical production per male worker continued upward in the 1950's, the value added in agriculture slumped. Rises in national income generated in agriculture were so small as to be more than offset by an increase in the male agricultural labor force of less than 1% per year. Even worse, from an expansion faster than population growth during the 1940's, increases in agricultural production, measured in either physical or value terms, dipped below those of the population during the 1950's.

The balance of trade in agricultural products reflected this more rapid increase in population than in food production. From deficits of about $10 million in agricultural trade during the early 1940's, imports rose swiftly. The average yearly trade deficit in agricultural products 1960–1962 was more than $80 million.[10] Scarce foreign exchange was thus dissipated on a consumers' good rather than spent for capital goods that would more directly stimulate the development effort.[11]

---

tistics, the average annual rate of growth of gross national product per capita in constant prices for Argentina was 1.17% from 1953 to 1960, for Brazil 0.73%, Mexico 2.48%, and Peru 0.73%. Meanwhile, for Chile, the rate was 0.16% when calculated using data from the same sources.

[8] The *National Accounts,* pp. 27–28, reveals them in turn.

[9] David Felix has described this effort and its outcome in "Structural Imbalances, Social Conflict, and Inflation: An Appraisal of Chile's Recent Antiinflationary Effort," *Economic Development and Cultural Change,* Vol. 8, No. 2 (January 1960), 113–147.

[10] Institute of Economics, *La economía de Chile,* II, 75, and Banco Central de Chile, *Boletín Mensual,* No. 426 (August 1963), 1048, 1061.

[11] Of course, food can spur capital formation directly when it is fed, say, to workers on public construction projects.

TABLE 1.2

CHILE: AGRICULTURAL PRODUCTION AND LABOR FORCE

	1940	1952	1960
Population, in thousands	5,023.5	5,933.0	7,375.2
Male agricultural labor force, in thousands	565.5	588.9	625.9
	1940–1942	1950–1952	1960–1962
Average yearly domestic income at factor prices generated in agriculture, in millions of 1961 escudos	371.3	465.5	487.6
Index of physical agricultural production	100.0	123.8	156.4
Annual rates of growth*	1940–1952	1952–1960	1940–1960
Population	1.39%	2.72%	1.92%
Male agricultural labor force	0.34	0.76	0.51
	1940/1942–1950/1952	1950/1952–1960/1962	1940/1942–1960/1962
Domestic income in agriculture	2.27	0.46	1.36
Domestic income generated in agriculture per male worker	1.86	−0.15	0.85
	1940–1950	1950–1959	1940–1959
Physical production	2.13	2.60	2.35
Physical production per male worker	1.73	1.92	1.82

* All rates of growth in this book are average annual rates of growth, continuously compounded.

Sources: Dirección de Estadística y Censos, *Cifras comparativas de los censos de 1940 y 1952 y muestra del censo de 1960* (Santiago, 1963); hereafter cited as *Cifras comparativas.* Corporación de Fomento, *National Accounts, op. cit.;* Institute of Economics, *La economía de Chile.*

The growth of industrial output, although considerably above that of agricultural products, nevertheless remained disappointingly low during the 1950's. Table 1.3 shows how the incentive effects on industrial production of wartime shortages and preferential foreign exchange rates during the 1940's gave way to more intense foreign competition and the near unification of the rates during the 1950's. Total income generated in manufacturing rose encouragingly at an annual rate of 6.5% during the 1940's, when population was growing about 1.4%, leaving an increase of more than 5% per year per capita. The situation during the 1950's changed abruptly, and the 5% figure fell to about a 1.3% rise in per capita domestic income generated in the manufacturing sector. Furthermore, the modern industrial sector did not grow to dominate manufacturing during the 1950's. In 1957, almost half the workers in the manufacturing labor force worked in firms employing fewer than five people.[12] The inability of the industrial sector to surpass the rate of population growth by a more comfortable margin set the tone for the performance of the rest of the economy during this period.

Finally, some evidence indicates that the distribution of income became more unequal during the inflationary period of the 1950's. The incomes of blue-collar workers and of members of the middle classes declined relative to those in the upper classes (*sector patronal*) from 1953 to 1959.[13] Between 1952 and 1960, the minimum salary (*sueldo vital*) paid to white-collar government workers rose by 10.9 times, while prices were climbing by 14.5 times.[14] This minimum salary influenced the amounts of wage readjustments made throughout the private economy to counteract inflation. At the bottom of the economic ladder, the minimum money wage for day laborers in agriculture rose by 7.0 times (1953–1960) at the same time as consumer prices were advancing by 11.5 times.[15]

An income distribution which is unequal and becoming increasingly so can be justified in only one way as a spur to development. Recipients of the highest incomes must save and invest the amounts which, in some sense, are warranted by these incomes. That they

---

[12] The industrial census of manufacturing firms with five or more employees shows 206,700 such workers in 1957. The 1952 and 1960 population censuses both counted about 405,000 workers in manufacturing enterprises of all sizes.

[13] Institute of Economics, *La economía de Chile*, I, 116.

[14] *Ibid.*, II, 1; Institute of Economics, *Desarrollo económico*, Table A-3; and Banco Central, *Boletín Mensual*, No. 426, 1042.

[15] Both the Institute of Economics publications cited in the previous note, and Banco Central, *Boletín Mensual*, No. 398, 395.

TABLE 1.3
CHILE: PRODUCTION AND LABOR FORCE IN MANUFACTURING

	1940	1952	1960
Population, in thousands	5,023.5	5,933.0	7,375.2
Manufacturing labor force, in thousands			
—male	192.6	274.3	303.7
—total	285.3	405.1	406.0
Average domestic income at factor prices generated in manufacturing, in millions of 1961 escudos	259.9	568.7	782.2
	1946	1953	1961
Industrial production indices*			
(1)	100.0	162.0	
(2)		100.0	127.5

Annual rates of growth	1940–1952	1952–1960	1940–1960
Population	1.39%	2.72%	1.92%
Manufacturing labor force			
—male	3.23	1.27	2.27
—total	2.92	0.03	1.76
Domestic income in manufacturing	6.53	3.99	5.51
Domestic income per worker in manufacturing	3.60	3.96	3.75

	1946–1953	1953–1961
Physical production in manufacturing	6.89%	3.04%

* These are two different series of physical production in manufacturing calculated by the Dirección de Estadística. Since the two differ in composition, the two series should not be spliced.

Sources: Same as for Table 1.2.

did not do so is clear from our examination of private capital formation and the data on agricultural and industrial output. If those people with the ability to make investments do not do so, then the development process would be stimulated far more by a more equal income distribution. Buoyant consumer goods markets and a relative decrease in the use of foreign exchange for imports of luxury consumer goods might have those growth-inducing effects on the economic system that the unequal income distribution accompanied by reluctance to save and invest failed to have.

In the chapters that follow, these conditions, present in the economy during the period in which migration was proceeding, will be coordinated with the nature of the migration itself. In the last chapter an ultimate attempt will be made to explain the observed migration and the economic stagnation in terms of one another, and a few guarded policy proposals will be added.

2

Migration – A Theoretical Picture

Internal migration can be thought of as part of a more general phenomenon: labor mobility. Labor mobility includes movements by workers among employers, occupations, industries, locations, or any combination of these. Internal migration may also involve a change of employer, occupation, or industry, but it need not. It must, however, by definition include a geographic movement. It is thus more specialized than labor mobility considered as a whole, but it may contain many of the same elements.[1]

Within the field of internal migration, attention most frequently centers on rural-urban migration. The customary characterization of urban migration involves a farm resident moving to the city. Past economic analyses of urban migration have been motivated by different sets of problems in the different parts of the world. In the United States, for instance, the "farm problem" — that is, the problem of low rural incomes — has been a target for economists' attention.[2] Near the other end of the development spectrum, the noisome living conditions of migrants in southern Asia have led to studies by UNESCO on some of the causes and effects of migration.[3]

---

[1] An introduction to some of the problems of labor mobility may be found in *Labor Mobility and Economic Opportunity*, a collection of essays by E. Wight Bakke *et al.* (New York: M.I.T. Press and Wiley, 1954).

[2] *Labor Mobility and Population in Agriculture*, published by the Iowa State University Center for Agricultural and Economic Adjustment (Ames, Iowa: Iowa State University Press, 1961), contains a number of essays dealing with this subject in detail.

[3] Research Centre on the Social Implications of Industrialization in Southern

The Theoretical Basis for Migration

Within a world of nineteenth-century economic theory, internal migration results from geographic differences in the productivity of labor. These differences are always reflected in wage differences, in this simple model. Assuming labor to be homogeneous, human flows have the double effect of tending to equalize marginal productivity among men and among regions. In this simplified scheme of atomistic firms, homogeneous labor and products, and a general atmosphere of flexibility and fluidity, equal marginal productivity also means equal wages.

Migration thus has a beneficial effect on over-all welfare in the economy. A worker moves only when his marginal product (wage) is higher at his destination than at his origin. Workers in the agricultural sector he leaves behind will also gain, since each of them will now be working with more land and capital. At the destination, however, the opposite will be true. Output per worker will fall marginally when the migrant becomes employed. With the application of a Heckscher-Ohlin-Stolper-Samuelson model, it can be shown that the disadvantaged workers may be bribed by those favorably affected and that a surplus will remain even after this act.[4] Over time, the response by migrants to economic opportunities should result in the disappearance of wage differentials. This conclusion about gains in welfare depends on assumptions that the wage and productivity differences which provoke the movement are themselves small, that the movement takes place with reasonable speed, and that the numbers of migrants involved are small in comparison with the total population. If these assumptions are not made, these happy results are not assured.

The gains to welfare through more fully realized economic development are present even when the model is complicated by relaxing the requirement that labor be homogeneous. If we imagine each region of a country having its own demand for differentiated and specialized workers, the flow of laborers of any given kind,

---

Asia, *The Social Implications of Industrialization and Urbanization: Five Studies of Urban Populations of Recent Rural Origin in Cities of Southern Asia* (Calcutta: UNESCO, 1956).

[4] Paul A. Samuelson, "Gains from Trade," *Canadian Journal of Economics and Political Science*, Vol. 5, No. 2 (May 1939), 195–205; Wolfgang Stolper and Paul A. Samuelson, "Protection and Real Wages," *Review of Economic Studies*, Vol. 9, No. 1 (November 1941), 58–73. Both were reprinted in American Economic Association, *Readings in the Theory of International Trade* (Philadelphia: Blakiston, 1950).

responding to regional wage (and presumably productivity) differentials, indicates an over-all increase in productivity and hence in welfare for the economy *as a whole*.[5]

What is the source of the geographical differences in marginal productivity of labor which provoke movement?

Even in the unlikely case of complete factor-and-product equilibrium in all parts of the country, differential fertility rates could upset the balance. If rural fertility rates were higher than urban, the resulting faster growth of rural population would change the assumed balance in population distribution. As these rural children aged and entered the labor force, the supply of rural labor would increase relative to the supply of urban labor. Then, assuming that other factors of production did not change, productivity differentials between countryside and town would arise, inducing migration.

The most obvious, almost tautological, spur to migration seems to be factor immobility — an immobility which allows differentials in factor productivity to form, as time passes. We can imagine a simple economy devoting all its energies to two activities, say, rural agriculture and urban industry. Labor productivity (and hence wages) may be low in agriculture because of capital immobility, shown by a hesitance to invest (in the pure sense of "create new capital") in agriculture. Even if the marginal productivity of capital is the same for agriculture and industry, the differences in labor productivity may still survive, owing to the reluctance of farm families to move to the city.

The causes of deep-seated factor immobility are especially difficult for the economist to discern and analyze. It seems certain that social attitudes play a large part in forming the relative degree of mobility. Even though they are qualified as being merely "social attitudes," they may at the same time be economically rational. For instance, they may tend toward the goal of maximizing the present value of lifetime income. Thus Professor Schultz and others picture migrants investing in the costs of moving in order to gain the returns of a higher wage at their destination. He suggests that older workers might be less prone to move, not because of sentimental ties to home, but because the pay-off period is shorter for them than for younger workers.[6]

Another important source of geographic differences in factor pro-

[5] The same sort of bribery mentioned in the preceding paragraph may be necessary, however.

[6] Theodore W. Schultz, "Investments in Human Capital," *American Economic Review*, Vol. 51, No. 1 (March 1961), 4, 14.

ductivity is the path which innovation takes within the economy. Technological changes in products, processes, marketing methods, organizational structure, or sources of raw materials will almost certainly alter the existing economic structure. Innovation does not occur at random, nor are its effects smoothly distributed over the whole economy. If mobility is anything less than perfect, there will be a period of productivity differentials after the introduction of an innovation into a perfectly equilibrated economy, followed by a period of adjustment of these differentials. This adjustment usually involves movement by people.

Interregional productivity differences may also result from a lack of information about opportunities in other areas. This information gap may be real, when media of communication among different regions are simply not sufficiently developed to transmit news of new conditions and changes. However, the lack of information may also reflect deeper cultural differences between city and countryside. Even when information is available, traditions, such as a tradition of illiteracy, may prevent its being received.

As a result of these barriers impeding movement, together with the dynamics of innovation and differential fertility rates, we may safely expect regional differences in labor productivity to continue in the future. This means, of course, that at least one of the incentives for migration — that of wage differentials — will also be present. Even in an economy as fluid as that of the United States, often used in the more underdeveloped countries as a model of flexibility and responsiveness to the price mechanism, these productivity and income differentials have persisted despite decades of well-established routes of migration.

Push and Pull

The causes for migration have long been thought to shed light on its effects.[7] Observers seeking the causes have usually been concerned with the welfare of the migrants themselves more directly than with the welfare of the whole society in which they lived. These writers have felt that when the motives for migration were known, policies could be formulated that would improve the conditions in which the migrants were living.

Two sorts of pressures have been hypothesized which could lead

---

[7] The International Labour Office has devoted one of its publications to the causes of urban migration. See *Why Labour Leaves the Land* (Geneva, 1960).

to migration from a rural setting to an urban one.[8] The first has been called the "push." The pressure of rural poverty, under this hypothesis, pushes the farmer off the land. The explanations for rural poverty are numerous. Low agricultural productivity forms the basis for many of these, but it is as unsatisfying as it is tautological to say that low agricultural productivity "causes" rural poverty. Depending on the observer, the low agricultural productivity, in turn, is blamed on lack of education and energy of the cultivators, or on land tenure arrangements that fail to provide incentives for capital improvements, or on government price policies that discourage investment in agriculture. Whatever may be the "correct" cause or combination of causes for low agricultural productivity, the result is the same. Low incomes in agriculture push farmers out of their rural pursuits and into the only alternative that exists for them: the city.

The second type of pressure on would-be migrants is the "pull" of more attractive urban opportunities. Opportunities can be defined quite broadly. The economist may tend to think first of job opportunities or chances for increased pay, but opportunities for education, entertainment, marriage, or even crime have also been considered in the literature.[9] The pull hypothesis can deal even with migration originating from comparatively rich rural regions. It says simply that the attractions of the city, in whatever form they may take for the migrant, are sufficient to pluck some people out of the rural population and deposit them in the city.

It seems clear that urban migration as found in the real world results from some combination of the "push" and "pull." These two hypotheses may be unified in one, in which urban migration is a function of expected rural-urban income differences. This of course implicitly makes the motivation for migration wholly economic. Nevertheless the combination of bleakness of rural prospects coupled with a more promising urban future is appealing as an explanation for migration.

It is hard to avoid skepticism about the results of certain empiri-

---

[8] It is not hard to extend these concepts to interurban migration as well as the more usual rural-urban migration.

[9] Samuel A. Stouffer, "Intervening Opportunities: A Theory Relating Mobility and Distance," *American Sociological Review*, Vol. 5, No. 6 (December 1940), 845–867; J. Matos Mar, "Migration and Urbanization — The 'Barriadas' of Lima: An Example of Integration into Urban Life" and Gino Germani, "Inquiry into the Social Effects of Urbanization in a Working-class Sector of Greater Buenos Aires," both in Philip M. Hauser, ed., *Urbanization in Latin America* (Paris: UNESCO, 1961), pp. 170–190 and 206–233.

cal studies which have tried to pinpoint more closely the causes for migration. For instance, a labor force survey of Greater Santiago asked the migrants their reasons for moving. Of all the migrants surveyed, 36% moved to Santiago because of better opportunities to obtain work, better pay in the same occupation, or an administrative transfer by their employer. Fifty-three per cent moved for "family" reasons. This number simply represents the number of wives and children who were born outside Santiago and accompanied the breadwinners in their moves. Finally, 5% came to Santiago as students, 4% for reasons classified as "various," and 2% were without data.[10]

This type of survey, while valuable in what it reveals, should be considered as showing only part of the whole picture. The respondents were not probed in any depth about their decision to move; their answers were fitted by the interviewers into six predetermined categories. Thus the nature of the answers themselves was predetermined. A survey of this type might lend itself speciously to an interpretation of migration which centered on economic factors and neglected the more broadly social background behind the migration. It is tempting to believe, for instance, that migrants do not perform complete economic analyses of their situations. Instead the city's bright lights or the absence of a suitable number of eligible spouses at home may be a powerful force inducing movement. When questioned later about his move, the migrant may rationalize his decision, especially when confronted by an interviewer who identifies himself with an institute of economics and who is forced to fit the migrants' answers into predetermined categories. The brevity of the interview and the closed-end questions narrow further the possibility of any but the most readily expected and easily classifiable answers.

Ravenstein and Redford

Historically, attention focused first on the internal migration experienced by the United Kingdom in response to its industrial revolution. The industrialization, although capital-intensive compared

[10] Ivan Yáñez, "Características principales de la migración hacia el Gran Santiago" (unpublished commercial engineering thesis, University of Chile, Faculty of Economic Sciences, 1958), pp. 27–31 and appendix tables 7–10, pp. 51–55. Most of the same material has also appeared in the more readily available publication of the Institute of Economics, *La población del Gran Santiago* (Santiago, 1959).

with the cottage industry prevalent before that time, nevertheless required labor to man the machines. At the same time, the enclosure movement was changing the nature of the agricultural sector of the economy, as landless farmers and their families were forced off their old holdings. This early combination of "pull" and "push," of employment opportunities in the towns and restrictive conditions in the rural areas, resulted in the first massive case of urban migration.

This early internal migration on a large scale did not possess the glamor or drama of international migration and hence did not attract the same analytical attention as did the overseas movement. E. G. Ravenstein conducted the first serious, detailed examination of British internal migration. He reported his results to an 1885 meeting of the Royal Statistical Society in a paper that is still widely cited.[11]

In this paper, Ravenstein examined empirically the currents of internal migration within the British Isles during the period between the censuses of 1871 and 1881. His work led him to the following conclusions:[12]

1. Most migration covered only short distances.
2. The migration proceeded by stages, one person filling the gap left by another who had moved earlier.
3. Each main current of migration produced a compensating countercurrent.[13]
4. Long distance movers generally went to big cities.
5. Town dwellers were less prone to move than were rural residents.
6. Females were more migratory than males.[14]

Arthur Redford, writing some forty years later, found Ravenstein's

---

[11] "The Laws of Migration," *Journal of the Royal Statistical Society*, Vol. 48, No. 2 (June 1885), 167–227. Ravenstein later extended his research on internal migration to the continent and North America, but did not alter substantially his earlier conclusions. The extended investigations appeared in the same journal, Vol. 52, No. 2 (June 1889), 241–301.

[12] Taken from the 1885 article, pp. 198–199.

[13] A contemporary example of this seemingly contradictory behavior can be found in the work of Larry Sjaastad, "The Costs and Returns of Human Migration," *Journal of Political Economy*, Vol. 70, No. 5, Part 2 (October 1962), especially p. 81, where he notes that "gross migration in one direction [is] the best single indicator of the amount of backflow." He takes the example of Mississippi, which lost 62,500 people during the year before the 1950 census, at the same time gaining 51,900 entrants to the state.

[14] In the 1889 article, this conclusion had become carefully qualified to read "Females appear to predominate among short-journey migrants" (p. 288).

generalizations valuable in his study of the human movement during the *first* half of the nineteenth century in Great Britain. His *Labour Migration in England, 1800–50* echoed Ravenstein on the wave- or stage-like character of the moves.[15] The migration was stimulated in part by the nature of the labor demand emanating from the new industrial towns. In general, "manufactories," turning out huge quantities of standardized goods, needed only unskilled "hands" to run the machines. Thus skill requirements were not stringent and migrants from rural areas were not excluded from the new jobs. We should note, by contrast, that the skill requirements in the industrial plants being formed in currently underdeveloped countries may be far more rigorous. Migrants without skill may thereby be shut out from employment in them.

Despite the high propensity for movement — Redford estimated that more than half the people living in the larger towns were born elsewhere — the countryside was not depopulated. Natural increase at least balanced losses by migration, and the enclosure movement extended itself to previously unused lands. Ashton notes that "no single county of England registered a decline of population between 1801 and 1851."[16]

Redford and Ravenstein were forthright in their praise of migration's effects. The process of migration shifted people from regions of lower economic opportunity to places where they might better contribute to the rise of the industrial society. At the same time their personal standard of living improved, as was the case with the migrants from rural England and Ireland. Ravenstein, in a concluding phrase whose tone reveals the century in which its author was writing, declared that "Migration means life and progress; a sedentary population stagnation."[17]

Behind this encomium lay the knowledge that the Industrial

[15] Manchester: University Press and London: Longmans, Green, 1926. For example, see p. 158.

[16] T. S. Ashton, *The Industrial Revolution 1760–1830* (London: Oxford University Press, 1948), p. 61. In France, on the other hand, a low birth rate was reflected in an absolute fall in rural population during the last quarter of the nineteenth century. Germany too underwent the same experience. Deficits in agricultural laborers caused in these countries by a rate of urban migration faster than the rate of rural natural increase were remedied in part by international immigration — from Belgium, Spain, and Italy to France and from Poland, Russia, Austria, and other East European countries to Germany. See J. H. Clapham, *Economic Development of France and Germany 1815–1914* (Cambridge: Cambridge University Press, 1961), pp. 167–170, 204–209.

[17] Ravenstein, 1889 article, *op. cit.*, p. 288.

Revolution represented a change so sweeping as to deserve the name "revolution," that urbanization was necessary for this industrialization, and that migration, in turn, provided the needed urban industrial workers. In the England of the nineteenth century, no "demonstration effects" or "revolution of rising expectations" accompanied these human flows to the towns, as they might in present underdeveloped countries. The common current problem of frustrated aspirations did not occur, simply because no previous examples of a more successful industrialization existed. We do not know how Ravenstein and Redford might have viewed urbanization unaccompanied by industrialization or, more specifically, unaccompanied by a sharp rise in manufacturing output. Nor do we know how they might have felt about an increasingly literate and politically sensitive urban proletariat, caught up in a national economic stagnation. But these were not the problems which faced early nineteenth-century England, nor were they the problems which faced Ravenstein and Redford as economic historians. They are the problems, however, which are typically posed today and to which I will direct some attention in the remainder of this work.

Schultz and Sjaastad

The most important work on migration which has recently appeared deals with migration as a form of investment in human capital. Unable to explain completely the sources of economic growth, especially when the most simple aggregates are used, viz., man-hours of labor and units of physical capital, economists have increasingly turned to expenditures which improve (in an economic sense) the quality of the human inputs into the economic process. Although concentrating their attention on education, these writers have also dealt with better health, on-the-job training, labor market information flows, and internal migration.[18]

Internal migration may be considered within a general model of investment in human capital. The costs of the investment, such as moving costs, must be compared with the returns, such as the income differentials accruing to the transferred workers. In a careful consideration of these costs and returns, Sjaastad has pointed out that more than direct costs and returns are involved.[19] Opportunity

---

[18] Much of this work was summarized and extended in a special issue of the *Journal of Political Economy*, Vol. 70, No. 5, Part 2 (October 1962).

[19] Sjaastad, *op. cit.*, pp. 80–93.

or nonmoney costs must also be taken into account if the causes and effects of migration are to be fully understood. Specifically, Sjaastad observes that the costs of migration should be equal to or less than the difference in the present value of the streams of earnings in the two different places. This means, of course, that interarea wage differentials could continue to exist without provoking migration, but only if they were smaller, in the sense just explained, than the costs of moving.

An examination of the specific items which comprise these costs and returns is revealing. Sjaastad divides these costs into two parts: money and nonmoney. Both types of cost may have more relevance for the analysis of movements in developed countries than in under-developed ones.

Money costs, for instance, are the *"increase* in expenditures for food, lodging, transportation (for both migrants and their belongings), etc."[20] But when migrants come to stay with friends or relatives, food and lodging costs may be miniscule. Transportation by truck is usually similarly inexpensive, as are second- and third-class railroad fares. Of course, when costs of movement are low, the wage differentials which spur the movement can be similarly low without lowering the *rate* of return on the investment which the migrant makes to put himself within striking distance of these more remunerative jobs.

The most important opportunity (nonmoney) costs will include "the earnings forgone while traveling, searching for, and learning a new job."[21] For a migrant from the countryside, these earnings forgone are likely to be very low. They will largely be in (difficult to measure) kind rather than in (easier to measure) money, which he will receive in the city. Furthermore, if there is unemployment outside the city, the simple "earnings forgone" may be zero if the migrant was previously unemployed, or close to zero if he was underemployed. Family incomes may also rise strikingly if females, formerly excluded from the labor force, are now able to get jobs.

Sjaastad also mentions the existence of psychic costs to migrants, which he cogently notes are not resource costs but may affect resource allocations. These costs usually include the disutility attached to leaving home and friends and putting oneself in an unfamiliar environment. Note, however, that the psychic cost of moving to a cosmopolitan capital from a backwoods hamlet may

[20] *Ibid.*, p. 83. Italics in original.
[21] *Ibid.*, p. 84.

well be negative. The strength of the attraction of the city's bright lights or the desire to escape from an unpleasant family situation in the village may be much stronger than the more frequently considered joys of home and hearthside.

These considerations all reinforce the point made earlier: that large flows of migration in the underdeveloped countries may well be economically justified without the presence of particularly significant wage differentials between geographic regions. Of course, once a tradition for migration is started, its effect is likely to be cumulative, since the probability will be even higher that any given person living outside the city knows someone who has moved. Since friends and relatives are sources of information and shelter, a snowball effect is likely to result once the number of migrants has grown to any substantial number.

The theoretical framework of Schultz and Sjaastad is further beset with data problems in the Chilean case. Chilean census data on economically meaningful gross migration cover only the total number of residents of each province born in each of the other provinces. No cross-classifying details of age, sex, occupation, or length of residence are available. Even if returns from migration could somehow be measured for Chile, comparing them with returns from investments in physical capital and other types of human capital would still be difficult.[22] These measurements have not been made and would be as difficult to make as the measurement of the return to migration.

Kuznets and Thomas

The final theoretical framework to be considered here is that of Simon Kuznets, Dorothy Swaine Thomas, and others, published in the American Philosophical Society's volumes *Population Redistribution and Economic Growth — United States, 1870–1950.*[23] There the relations between the processes of internal migration and economic development are explored at length. On the one hand, the presence of economic opportunity acts upon the distribution of population. "The distribution of a country's population at any given time may be viewed as a rough adjustment to the distribution of

[22] This strict comparison of costs and returns has been sharply criticized by R. S. Eckhaus in "Investment in Human Capital: A Comment," *Journal of Political Economy,* Vol. 71, No. 5 (October 1963), 501–504.
[23] Three volumes. Philadelphia; 1957, 1960, and 1964.

economic opportunities."[24] How do we know that population distribution has been responsive to economic opportunities? For the United States, the notable convergence over time in per capita incomes and economic structure among the states and regions furnishes some corroborative evidence.[25]

On the other hand, how does the internal migration itself stimulate economic development? Here the answer lies in its demographic selectivity.

> There are marked migration differentials by sex, age, race, family status, education, health, and many other social and demographic characteristics; and . . . migrants, especially those moving long distances and between highly dissimilar environments, are probably preselected . . . for their capacity to detach themselves from traditional surroundings. For these reasons the jobward migrating components of the population may be among the most productive from the standpoint of economic growth. Not only do they tend to be in the demographic brackets that assure comparatively full productive power, but their very rootlessness may promote adjustment to new opportunities.[26]

Thus the full circularity of cause and effect (1) between economic opportunity and its stimulus to population redistribution and (2) between this redistribution and its effect on subsequent growth is explored.

In the work which follows, the migration selectivity (the second branch of this two-branched circle of reasoning) can be fairly well documented in the Chilean case. On the other hand, data on regional structure of the economy and on wages and their interregional differentials were simply not available. In a country where there are even fewer economic data than in the United States, the construction of regional economic data would be an even more forbidding task than it was for the Kuznets and Thomas exploration party, who had the advantage of working with relatively well-developed economic data for the United States.

The following chapters will try to blend the elements set forth in this chapter into a composite applicable to the migration empirically exhibited by Chile. The "push" and "pull," applications of the Redford-Ravenstein hypotheses, the costs-and-returns framework of

---

[24] Ibid., I, 2.
[25] See Richard Easterlin's chapter, "Regional Growth of Income: Long Term Tendencies" in Kuznets and Thomas, op. cit., II, 141–183.
[26] Kuznets and Thomas, op. cit., I, 3.

Schultz and Sjaastad, and the emphasis on demographic selectivity of Kuznets and Thomas can all be related to the Chilean migration of the past two decades. Within the constraints that data problems place upon the analysis, each of these ingredients will be judiciously reviewed for its possible contribution to an enlarged understanding of the problems of urban migration in an underdeveloped country.

3

Centralization
of Economic Activity

Some students of urbanization and of the economic development
which may accompany it allege that within any given country the
cities should order themselves in a specified size distribution in
order that certain imbalances be avoided. They claim that if too
many people live in the largest city or too few in middle-sized cities,
then the processes of economic and social development will not
proceed in the orderly fashion that a more balanced city-size distribution might encourage.

The city-size distribution considered most "normal" or "balanced"
is that given by the rank-size rule. Ranking a nation's cities by population size, the rule says that the second largest city should have
a population half as large as the largest city, the third largest should
have one-third the population of the largest, and so on. The normal
character associated with this rule stems from studies of U.S. city-
size distribution, perhaps best summarized by Professor Walter
Isard.[1]

At least two possible objections exist to the rank-size rule as a test
for balance of city-size distributions. The first concerns its empirical
validity. Isard himself sagely notes, "How much validity and uni-
versality should be attributed to this rank-size rule is . . . a matter

[1] *Location and Space-Economy* (New York: Technology Press and Wiley,
1956), Chapter 3. More specifically, the rule says
$$rP^q = K$$
where r is the city's population rank, P its population, and q and K constants
for the group of cities being tested.

of individual opinion and judgment."[2] The rule's failures, for instance, in the United States and the Soviet Union at a number of twentieth-century dates have been documented by Frederick Moore.[3]

The second objection is even more important. Of what economic significance is a city-size distribution conforming to the rank-size rule? The observers who find the largest city too large or the smaller cities too small, using the rule as their criterion for judging this balance, many times claim or imply that an imbalance so defined has detrimental economic effects. A typical passage reads as follows: "*Over-concentration* of the urban population in relatively few cities, rather than 'over-urbanization' *per se*, appears more serious and likely to emerge as the key bottleneck in any program of industrialization."[4] Just why "over-concentration" represents such a handicap to development is usually not made clear. The suspicion lurks, of course, that the city-size distribution of the developed countries, presumably dictated or predicted by the rank-size rule, is assumed to be the norm to which the currently developing countries should aspire. Countries that do not exhibit the balance defined by the rank-size rule should seek to achieve that balance.

An economic justification for the sort of balance represented by the rank-size criterion might be revealed by an examination of the market and transportation processes in an extensively agricultural country in the process of development. An example is the United States during the mid-nineteenth century. The network of towns of progressively and evenly spaced diminishing size could have been dictated by early gaps in transportation — gaps which necessitated population agglomerations of smoothly graduated size to handle the flows both of primary goods from the smallest towns to the metropolises and of manufactured articles in the opposite direction. The decentralization of government and administration during this phase of development might also be explained by the high costs of information which primitive communication arrangements caused.

In mid-twentieth century, many of the economic justifications for

[2] *Ibid.*, p. 57.

[3] "A Note on City Size Distribution," *Economic Development and Cultural Change*, Vol. 7, No. 4 (July 1959), 465–466.

[4] Janet L. Abu-Lughod, "Urbanization in Egypt: Present State and Future Prospects," *Economic Development and Cultural Change*, Vol. 13, No. 3 (April 1965), 315. Emphasis in original.

this sort of balance would have been removed. In particular, the decreased costs of transportation and communication would have obviated the need for continuity in the series of decreasing sized staging-and-information-collecting points. Even in currently under-developed countries, despite their backwardness in economic infra-structure, the economic justification for a city-size distribution based on the rank-size rule may well have been eliminated by the potentials which modern transportation and communication hold.

In short, the reliance on the rank-size rule as a norm seems strained. Its economic justification is at best dated and at worst suggests that underdeveloped countries should imitate slavishly those patterns of growth which the currently developed countries underwent during the past century. Even more conclusively, Brian J. L. Berry notes, after a detailed empirical study, that

> there are no relationships between type of city size distribution and either relative economic development or the degree of urbanization of countries, although urbanization and economic development are highly associated.[5]

Centralization in Latin America

The rapid rate of urbanization and population growth in Latin America culminates in the swollen size of the capitals of many of these countries. In contrast to the United States and Canada, where the capitals have been located in smaller cities, only two of Latin America's republics — Brazil and Ecuador — have the central seat of government outside the largest city.[6] In all the others, the centers of economic, educational, cultural, and diplomatic functions are concentrated in the capital city.

Historically the capital cities were centers of the colonial adminis-tration. Mexico City, Lima, Bogotá, and Buenos Aires were all designated as capitals of vice-royalties; Quito, Santiago, and

[5] "City Size Distribution and Economic Development," *Economic Develop-ment and Cultural Change*, Vol. 9, No. 4, Part 1 (July 1961), 587.

[6] In Ecuador, the port of Guayaquil has grown at the rate of 5.5% per year (1950–1960) to overtake the population of historic Quito. In Brazil, São Paulo has exhibited a similarly dramatic rate of urban growth, surpassing the former capital of Rio de Janeiro. Meanwhile, Brazil's capital has been removed to the newly created Brasília. These are Latin America's only two countries in which the processes of natural population increase and internal migration have been stronger outside the capital than within it.

Panama as heads of captaincies-general or presidencies. In addition to their civil roles, many of the same cities also acted as archbishoprics or lesser centers of religious administration. Thus the stage was set early for their importance during the postcolonial period.

Administrative centralism, begun under Spanish rule, was continued in Latin America after the republics had won their independence. The colonial period's capitals became national capitals, and the experience of the people with the centralized administration of government was reflected in the size and power of these capitals of the newly independent countries. The present population of the capital cities and of their nations is shown in Table 3.1.

The centralized nature of some of these countries is clearly indicated in these figures. In Chile, Argentina, and Uruguay, at least one out of every four citizens lives in the capital. On the other hand, in Colombia and Brazil and perhaps in Peru and Ecuador as well, the largest city is no larger relative to the size of the country than in the United States and Canada.

One index of urbanization is the percentage of a country's people living in towns of more than 20,000 people. The presence of a huge capital city inflates this urban index greatly. The percentage of Argentinians, Chileans, and probably of Uruguayans living in urban centers of more than 20,000 was double that of Colombia, Brazil, Peru, and Ecuador in the early 1950's.[7]

Urban centralization not only implies a city large in proportion to the country supporting it, but also the absence of any other cities of comparable size. The rank-size rule, on the other hand, implies that the population of the second and third largest cities, plus a fraction (one-sixth) of the population of the fourth largest, should equal the population of the largest city. The table on page 28 shows the quotient of the capital's (or largest city's) population divided by this sum. Rank-size "balance" is shown by a quotient close to one; higher quotients indicate capital cities which are large relative to the next largest cities.[8]

---

[7] United Nations, Economic Commission for Latin America, "The Demographic Situation in Latin America," *Economic Bulletin for Latin America*, Vol. 6, No. 2 (October 1961), 32–35.

[8] Calculated from data in United Nations Economic Commission for Latin America, "Geographic Distribution of the Population of Latin America and Regional Development Priorities," *Economic Bulletin for Latin America*, Vol. 8, No. 1 (March 1963), 59.

TABLE 3.1

CENTRALIZATION OF POPULATION — INTERNATIONAL COMPARISONS

Country	Capital*	1960 Population†			1950 Population†		
		Nation	Capital	Capital as Per Cent of Nation	Nation	Capital	Capital as Per Cent of Nation
Argentina	Buenos Aires	20,956	7,000	33.4%	17,189	5,100	29.7
Bolivia	La Paz	3,696	450‡	12.2	3,013	320	10.6
Brazil	São Paulo*	70,600	3,250	4.6	51,976	2,017	3.9
Chile	Santiago	7,627	1,900	24.9	6,073	1,275	21.0
Colombia	Bogotá	15,468	1,118	7.2	11,679	620	5.3
Ecuador	Guayaquil*	4,317	450	10.4	3,197	259	8.1
Paraguay	Asunción	1,768	311	17.6	1,397	219	15.7
Peru	Lima–Callao	10,857	1,875	17.3	8,521	1,075	12.6
Uruguay	Montevideo	2,827	1,150‡	40.7	2,407	935‡	38.8
Venezuela	Caracas	7,331	1,250	17.1	4,974	694	14.0
Mexico	Mexico	34,988	4,666	13.3	25,826	2,884	11.2
Cuba	Havana	6,797	1,600‡	23.5	5,508	1,080	19.6
Canada	Montreal	17,909	2,110§	11.8	13,712	1,395‖	10.2
United States	New York	180,676	14,115	7.8	152,271	12,296	8.1

* Or largest city.
† In thousands. Population of the whole metropolitan area, not just the city proper.
‡ Estimate very rough.
§ 1961
‖ 1951

Sources: U.N. Demographic Yearbook 1962, 1960, and 1955; Economic Commission for Latin America, "Geographic Distribution of the Population of Latin America and Regional Development Priorities," Economic Bulletin for Latin America, Vol. 8, No. 1 (March 1963), 58–59. Note that for Chile and for some other countries as well, these estimates of population differ from those reported by the national census.

Country	Date	Quotient[9]	Country	Date	Quotient[9]
Argentina	1947	4.8	Ecuador	1950	0.96
Bolivia	1950	1.6	Mexico	1950	3.6
Brazil	1960	0.47	Paraguay	1950	5.3
Chile	1952	3.3	Peru	1961	7.1
Colombia	1951	0.83	Venezuela	1961	1.7
Cuba	1953	3.7			

The extent of centralization in Chile, Argentina, Cuba, Mexico, Peru, and Paraguay is apparent from the table. One city clearly predominates within the city-size distribution. This, of course, is reminiscent of Mark Jefferson's concept of primate cities.[10] He defined the primate city variously as the capital, the largest city, the leading market, and the center of national influence. To qualify as a primate city, the capital had to have only twice as many people as the next largest city. Furthermore, no relation was postulated by Jefferson between the size of the capital and the population of its nation, or between their relative rates of growth.

It is to this last aspect of centralization that we turn next. One might postulate that in a country undergoing urban centralization the largest city would be growing considerably faster than other smaller cities and faster than the country as a whole. Table 3.2 shows that expansion of population in the capitals at double the national rates of population growth is not uncommon. Since the over-all population of Latin America is growing at a rate faster than any of the world's other continents, the growth of the capitals *as a multiple* of their countries' growth is even more striking.

Bolivia seems to be the only South American exception to this generalization about rapid urban growth. La Paz grew at a rate less than Bolivia's between 1942 and 1957. The violence and economic disorganization following the Bolivian revolution in 1952 probably triggered the same back-to-the-farm movement experienced in other countries during similar periods of social unrest.[11]

The striking recent growth of the Latin American capitals attests

[9] Quotient = $\dfrac{\text{population of largest city}}{\substack{\text{sum of population of second and third largest cities and}\\ \text{one-sixth the population of the fourth largest city}}}$

[10] "The Law of the Primate City," *Geographical Review*, Vol. 29, No. 2 (April 1939), 226–232.

[11] One of a plethora of articles describing the Bolivian revolution and its aftermath is Richard W. Patch's "Bolivia: U.S. Assistance in a Revolutionary Setting" in Council on Foreign Relations, *Social Change in Latin America Today* (New York: Vintage Books, 1961), 108–176.

TABLE 3.2
GROWTH OF POPULATION IN NATIONS AND THEIR CAPITALS*

Country	Period	Growth of Capital*	Growth of Nation	Capital City Growth Rate Divided by National Growth Rate
Argentina	1947–1960	2.1%	1.8%	1.17
Bolivia	1942–1957	0.8	1.3	0.63
Brazil	1940–1960	5.1	2.3	2.17
Chile	1940–1960	3.5	1.9	1.85
Colombia	1951–1959	6.9	2.2	3.12
Ecuador	1950–1960	5.5	3.0	1.86
Paraguay	1950–1960	3.5	2.3	1.49
Peru	1940–1960	4.4	2.2	2.04
Uruguay	—	—	—	—
Venezuela	1941–1959	7.4	3.0	2.46
Mexico	1940–1960	5.4	2.8	2.07
Cuba	1943–1953	4.4	2.0	2.21
Canada	1941–1961	3.1	2.2	1.11
United States	1940–1960	1.0	1.5	0.68

* Or largest city.

Sources: United Nations, *Demographic Yearbook 1960* and *1962;* Chile, 1960 preliminary census results; International Urban Research, *The World's Metropolitan Areas* (Berkeley, 1958); Laura Randall, "Labour Migration and Mexican Economic Development," *Social and Economic Studies,* Vol. 11, No. 1 (March 1962), 73–81.

to their magnetic attraction for internal migrants. Bigness and growth tend to generate further size and faster growth, as Table 3.1 showed. A partial explanation was touched on in Chapter 2: the presence of a group of friends and relatives in the city implies lower costs of migration for those still outside, taking "costs" in a very broad sense.[12] An ever bigger group of urban acquaintances spreads the word among more people back home. The process merely requires each migrant to attract, on the average, one additional migrant to the city in order to be self-generating. Naturally the shorter the time lag between the arrival of a migrant and the subsequent arrivals of his friends and relatives, the faster city population will expand.

[12] Philip Nelson has cast an analysis of American internal migration in terms of the number of friends and relatives already living in the place of destination. He found this more significant (mathematically) than relationships between migration and income differentials or between migration and unemployment differentials. See his unpublished doctoral dissertation, "A Study in the Geographic Mobility of Labor," Columbia University, 1957, and a later article, "Migration, Real Income, and Information," *Journal of Regional Science,* Vol. 1, No. 2 (Spring 1959), 43–74.

We might hypothesize that the biggest capitals would also be those growing most rapidly. The data, however, refute this guess. During the 1950's, neither a positive nor negative relationship is apparent. Some small capitals grew slowly (Asunción) while some grew more rapidly (Bogotá, Caracas). Some large capitals grew slowly (Buenos Aires) while some grew more rapidly (Mexico City).

More promising is the hypothesis that the capital grows in an inverse relation to its relative size. Relatively small capitals, i.e., capitals small relative to the population of their countries, will grow at more rapid rates than relatively large capitals. Such an hypothesis might be justified by reasoning that there is a limit to the relative number of a country's population who can be supported in the capital by the rest of the country, and that as this limit is approached, growth of the capital will become slower. This hypothesis fares better than the previous one at the hands of the data: the squared coefficient or correlation (r^2) between relative size of the capital in 1950 and rate of population growth in the capital during the period from 1950 to 1960 is 0.69, which is significant at the 5% level.[13] If this trend were to continue in the future, we would expect growth in the relatively large capitals of Uruguay, Argentina, Chile, and Cuba to be slower than that of the relatively smaller capitals, say, in Colombia and Mexico.

Centralism in Chile

The preceding section has demonstrated that Chile, although not the most centralized of the Latin American nations, has a comparatively high degree of centralism. More than a quarter of the people live in Santiago; the next largest urban complex, the metropolitan Valparaíso–Viña del Mar area, contains only a fifth as many people, and over the past twenty years Santiago has grown almost twice as fast as the country as a whole.

The speed of Santiago's growth with respect to smaller towns is detailed in Table 3.3. Among places with more than 10,000 people, Santiago grew faster than towns of any other size. The two centers with between 100,000 and 1,000,000 inhabitants (Valparaíso–Viña

---

[13] This correlation uses data for Mexico, Cuba, and the South American countries except Bolivia. It seemed wise to exclude Bolivia as an "exceptional" case, for reasons noted in the text, p. 28.

del Mar and Concepción), on the other hand, did not even match the over-all national rate of population increase.

TABLE 3.3

CHILE: POPULATION CHANGES, BY SIZE OF CITY

Size of City in 1960	Population, in Thousands		
	1940	1952	1960
More than 1,000,000 (Santiago)	952	1,350	1,907
100,000–1,000,000	362	424	517
50,000–100,000	379	441	570
20,000–50,000	378	517	718
10,000–20,000	189	247	333
"Urban" towns with less than 10,000*	376	594	845
"Rural" areas*	2,388	2,360	2,485
Total population	5,024	5,933	7,375
All towns with less than 10,000	2,764	2,954	3,330

Size of City in 1960	Annual Rate of Growth of Population		
	1940–1952	1952–1960	1940–1960
More than 1,000,000 (Santiago)	2.9%	4.3%	3.5%
100,000–1,000,000	1.3	2.5	1.8
50,000–100,000	1.3	3.2	2.0
20,000–50,000	2.6	4.1	3.2
10,000–20,000	2.2	3.8	2.8
"Urban" towns with less than 10,000*	3.8	4.4	4.1
"Rural" areas*	−0.1	0.6	0.2
Total population	1.4	2.7	1.9
All towns with less than 10,000	0.5	1.5	0.9

* "Urban" and "rural" are defined according to census criteria, which classify as "urban" areas those towns with "urban characteristics." For the complete definition see Servicio Nacional de Estadística y Censos, *XII censo general de población* (Santiago, 1956), I, 67.

Source: Unpublished data of the Dirección de Estadística y Censos.

Only small towns with "urban characteristics," but fewer than 10,000 people, grew faster than Santiago. The rapid growth of population in these towns may only reflect census reclassifications of previously "rural" towns as "urban," especially for the 1960 census. Population growth in all places (rural and urban) of less than 10,000 was less than a quarter of that for the urban areas under 10,000.

The dramatic recent growth of Santiago and the seemingly inevitable centralization of a broad range of activities there have served as a powerful stimulant to political invective. A typical example appears in the proceedings of a youth congress held in 1963 by one of the opposition parties. The congress dealt with problems on which youth hoped to make constructive criticisms and contributions. In addition to the areas of labor, international relations, and land tenure, they included *el centralismo*.

The youth defined centralism as "hypertrophied development of public and private institutions, which results in the concentration of industrial, commercial, educational, or political and other activities within a given region in a country, generally its capital." Warming to their subject, they declared in the next sentence that "there is no doubt whatever that Chile at present is affected by the crisis of centralism." Their conclusions were that "centralism in all its forms is becoming progressively worse at an accelerated rate" and that "with each passing day the provinces participate less in the various national activities."[14] In the rest of this chapter we will examine some aspects of centralism in employment, government spending, and growth-oriented investment in Chile to try to determine the validity of these charges.

Employment

Data from the 1960 census and from sample surveys of employment near the census date emphasize the degree to which the labor market as a whole and the industrial labor market in particular center their activities in Santiago. As Table 3.4 shows, more than a quarter of the Chilean labor force of 2.2 million was found in Santiago in 1960. In manufacturing, construction, commerce, and services, the fraction in Santiago ranged between one-half and one-third. Furthermore, if we consider the entire work force in the twelve biggest urban centers outside Santiago, we find only slightly more than half the number of workers found in Santiago alone, according to estimates derived from census data.

The startling inequality in size between the largest labor market and the next largest ones leads us to seek an explanation for these differences. If, for instance, unemployment in Santiago were significantly lower than in other urban centers, the reasons for Santiago's faster population growth would be far clearer. For residents of other large towns, the pressures exerted by unemployment could be partially relieved by going to Santiago, while for those living outside

[14] Segundo Congreso Nacional de la Juventud Demócrata Christiana, *Informe* (Santiago, 1963), p. 31.

big towns and considering a move to any one of them, Santiago would be the most attractive.

Unfortunately for ease of analysis, this does not seem to have been the case. Table 3.5 gives estimates of unemployment in Greater

TABLE 3.4

SANTIAGO'S RELATIVE POSITION AS AN INDUSTRIAL CENTER, 1960

	Industrial Distribution of Labor Force (in Thousands)				
	Chile	San-tiago	Valparaíso–Viña del Mar	Concep-ción	Six Other Cities
Agriculture	648.0	15.0	0.9	0.6	2.6
Mining and quarrying	97.3	3.8	0.8	0.3	4.3
Manufacturing	406.0	187.2	30.0	15.6	14.7
Construction	164.5	55.0	5.9	3.3	11.8
Commerce	225.3	98.7	23.0	9.6	15.5
Transportation, storage, communication, public utilities	120.2	35.0	11.9	6.9	13.2
Government and finance			23.6	3.6	8.0
Personal services	568.4	225.9	29.9	11.3	13.8
"Other" services			15.8	7.1	13.5
Activities not well specified*	126.3	44.6	1.2	0.5	2.5
Total	2,356.0	665.2	143.0	58.7	99.9

	Industrial Distribution by Percentages				
	Chile	San-tiago	Valparaíso–Viña del Mar	Concep-ción	Six Other Cities
Agriculture	27.5%	2.3%	0.6%	1.0%	2.6%
Mining and quarrying	4.1	0.6	0.6	0.5	4.3
Manufacturing	17.2	28.1	21.0	26.6	14.7
Construction	7.0	8.3	4.1	5.6	11.8
Commerce	9.6	14.8	16.1	16.4	15.5
Transportation, storage, communication, public utilities	5.1	5.3	8.3	11.8	13.2
Government and finance			16.5	6.1	8.0
Personal services	24.1	34.0	20.9	19.3	13.8
"Other" services			11.0	12.1	13.5
Activities not well specified*	5.4	6.7	0.8	0.9	2.5
Total	100.0	100.0	100.0	100.0	100.0

TABLE 3.4 (*Continued*)

	Percentage of Each Industry's Labor Force Present in Certain Cities			
	Santiago	Valparaíso–Viña del Mar	Concepción	Six Other Cities
Agriculture	2.3%	0.1%	0.1%	0.4%
Mining and quarrying	3.9	0.8	0.3	4.4
Manufacturing	46.1	7.4	3.8	3.6
Construction	33.4	3.6	2.0	7.2
Commerce	43.8	10.2	4.3	6.9
Transportation, storage, communication, public util.	29.1	9.9	5.7	11.0
Government, finance, personal and "other" services	39.7	12.2	3.8	6.2
All economic activities	28.2%	6.1%	2.5%	4.2%

* Includes those seeking work for the first time.

Notes: The figures represent the following dates — Chile and Santiago, 29 November 1960; Valparaíso–Viña del Mar, September 1960; Concepción, December 1960; six other cities, March 1961. The six are Valdivia, Antofagasta, Iquique, La Serena-Coquimbo, Puerto Montt, and Castro.

Sources: Instituto de Economía, *Ocupación y desocupación*, No. 57 (March 1963); No. 53 (Sept., 1962); Dirección de Estadística, *Algunos resultados del XIII censo* (Santiago, 1963).

Santiago and other surveyed cities at two different dates. Santiago did not present a brighter employment picture than most of the other towns surveyed in March 1961. Two and one-half years later, the outlook had changed only for a group of towns in a five-province area in the south-central part of the country.[15] Here, Santiago's unemployment was significantly lower than any of the towns in this region. The poor labor market conditions there reflected regional characteristics: a lack of dynamism in the local coal mines, a somewhat larger concentration of Indians there than in the rest of the country, and the nationally prevalent inability of agriculture to modernize. Thus if migrants were fully aware of the unemployment situation in the various cities of Chile, they would not choose Santiago for its overwhelming superiority in this respect. In turn, we cannot blame the centralization of the labor market in Santiago on more favorable urban unemployment rates there.[16]

[15] The provinces were Arauco, Bío-Bío, Concepción, Malleco, and Ñuble.
[16] The finding that migration to Santiago has continued in the face of equal measured unemployment between Santiago and other cities is consistent with the finding that migration did not increase as unemployment in Santiago fell. See Chapter 5.

TABLE 3.5
CHILE: UNEMPLOYMENT, 95% CONFIDENCE LIMITS*

City	March 1961 Upper Limit	Lower Limit
Iquique	9.9%	4.7%
Antofagasta	10.3	5.7
La Serena-Coquimbo	11.4	8.8
Greater Santiago	8.4	6.8
Concepción	8.2	5.8
Valdivia	11.2	8.4
Puerto Montt	8.1	5.7
Castro	7.3	4.9

City	September 1963 Upper Limit	Lower Limit
Greater Santiago	5.8%	4.6%
Valparaíso–Viña del Mar	4.6	3.0
Concepción (city only)	6.1	4.1
In a five-province region: †		
Chillán	9.5	6.7
Concepción-Talcahuano	8.4	6.0
Lota-Coronel	13.0	9.6
Total urban in the region	10.2	8.0
Total rural in the region	8.6	6.0
Total region	9.0	7.2

* The probability is 0.95 that true unemployment falls between the upper and lower limits shown.

† Including the provinces of Arauco, Bío-Bío, Concepción, Malleco, and Ñuble.

Sources: Ocupación y desocupación (Santiago, Instituto de Economía, March 1961 and September 1963).

Government Spending

The central government can further the centralization process by concentrating its expenditures within Santiago.[17] Or if it favors decentralization, its spending can reinforce that preference. Within a democratic government, however, many obstacles may interfere with the completion of a desired policy. Even if enunciation of national goals always resulted in action, the lack of a clear political consensus about these goals frequently intrudes. With the legisla-

[17] The importance of the central government in fiscal affairs is attested to by the Inter-American Development Bank: "The taxing system [in Chile] is highly centralized, with municipal taxes averaging less than 6% of Central Government collections and the provinces being entirely without tax revenues." Presumably spending ability closely follows taxing ability. Institutional Reforms and Social Development Trends in Latin America (Washington, D.C., 1963), p. 102.

ture controlling most spending, regional appropriations are far more likely to reflect a complex combination of political bargains than any consciously sought national goals. In Chile, the absence of regional accounting for government expenditures makes regional policy, even if clearly formulated and legislatively approved, difficult to carry out.

School construction expenditures are one of the few types of government spending with available regional data. Table 3.6 shows the 1963 budgeted amounts for completion of schools already under construction or to be initiated in that year. School construction expenditures influence economic events beyond their mere regional multiplier effects. If children in rural areas are taught farm skills they are far more likely as young adults to be strongly attached to the land than if they come in daily from the fields to receive courses

TABLE 3.6

CHILE: PUBLIC SCHOOL CONSTRUCTION, BUDGETS, BUILDINGS INITIATED
OR IN PROGRESS, 1963

| Type of School | Amounts in Thousands of Escudos | | |
	Greater Santiago	Outside Santiago	Total Chile
Primary	2,770	13,952	16,722
Secondary	1,544	3,141	4,686
Vocational — urban	405	4,692	5,097
Vocational — rural	—	945	945
Total	4,720	22,731	27,450

| Type of School | Percentage of National Total | | |
	Greater Santiago	Outside Santiago	Total Chile
Primary	16.6%	83.4%	100.0%
Secondary	33.0	67.0	100.0
Vocational — urban	7.9	92.1	100.0
Vocational — rural	—	100.0	100.0
Total	17.2%	82.8%	100.0%
Number of children under fifteen years old, in thousands	728.6	2,205.8	2,934.4
Per cent of national total	24.8%	75.2%	100.0%

Notes: "Vocational — urban" includes the following types of schools: normal, industrial, commercial, técnica femenina. "Vocational — rural" includes escuelas rurales and an escuela granja. Secondary schools include colegios medios and liceos.

Source: República de Chile, Inversión pública 1963 (Santiago, 1962), VI, 8–76.

in machine tending. The data, however, indicate that despite the concentration of nearly half of Chile's manufacturing activity in Santiago, only 7.9% of the amounts budgeted for vocational schools were planned for Greater Santiago. Only one public industrial school was being constructed there in 1963.

At the opposite end of the educational spectrum, one-third of the money to be spent for construction of secondary school buildings was scheduled for Santiago. Chilean secondary education has emphasized classical and humanistic studies at the expense of the experimental and empirical sciences. Thus while children outside Santiago were being specifically trained in vocational skills, Santiago emphasized the arts and letters. Until investment in the provinces provides physical capital to complement the industrial skills being taught there, additional migration to Santiago can be the only result.

The other component of government expenditures for which regional data are available is the public housing program of the Housing Corporation (Corporación de la Vivienda, CORVI). In 1961, CORVI calculated a housing priority for each of 137 cities and towns, in addition to estimating the absolute deficiency in numbers of dwellings in each place.[18] In general, the larger the city, the higher the deficiency and the higher the housing priority. Places with higher priorities, in general, were scheduled to make up a greater proportion of their deficiencies. For instance, the Greater Santiago area with its high priority and an estimated deficiency of about 115,000 dwellings was to have 37,000 built during the plan; roughly one-third of its deficiency was to be remedied during the years 1962–1964. On the other hand, the very small towns with the lowest priorities only would erase about one-tenth of their deficiencies under the plan.[19]

---

[18] Details on the housing deficiencies, priorities, and plans to remove these deficiencies are given in CORVI, Departamento de Planeamiento y Estudios Económicos, *1962–1964 2? Plan Trienal* (Santiago, 1961). The priorities were a complicated weighted index, including the following factors for each of the 137 places considered: number of urban inhabitants; inhabitants of "deficient" and "bad" housing according to a standard classification; substandard buildings such as *rucas, ranchos, callampas,* and *conventillos;* family heads receiving wages and salaries and living in "deficient" and "bad" houses; deficient and bad houses with crowding (*hacinamiento*); one- and two-room houses with crowding; population increase 1952–1961; houses destroyed in a 1960 earthquake; and finally the probable housing deficiency in 1961. See *Plan*, pp. 18, 59–60.

[19] The ten cities with priorities above 10 on CORVI's scale were slated to have an average 32.8% of their deficiencies removed, according to the three-

The effects of these policies on further centralization are easy to discern. Santiago had a huge housing shortage, both in absolute terms and relative to its population. The Housing Corporation, however, proposed to remedy a high proportion of this deficit in dwellings. If a sizable stream of migrants were attracted to a pre-CORVI Santiago — one with an almost desperate housing shortage — then the size of the stream would not grow smaller as the shortage was eased.

Thus the public school construction program and the public housing program both tended to lead to further centralization of population and economic activity.

The Chilean Development Corporation

One other public institution deserves attention in a review of influences on centralization. The Corporación de Fomento de la Producción (CORFO) was established in 1939 to spur reconstruction following an earthquake and to stimulate the economic development of the country in general.[20] Within the government, CORFO occupies a key position. As a semiautonomous public body, on whose board sit both government and private officials, it is charged with the preparation of Chilean development plans. In the past it has also been active in direct investment in new firms.

As the public body most oriented to change, CORFO differs from other Chilean government groups, for which inertia and political pressures are probably more important in determining volume and composition of expenditures than are any systematic studies. CORFO has the responsibility for development measures — measures which by their nature involve fairly thorough preliminary studies and subsequent choices among available development alternatives. The responsibility for long-range planning forces upon CORFO a perspective not found in the rest of the public sector.

For this reason, the nature of CORFO's investment choices over the years since its founding have more interest than their mere

---

year plan. In contrast, the towns with priorities lower than 4, none of which had more than 10,000 residents in 1960, were only to make up 10.7% of their housing deficiencies according to the plan.

[20] The best publication about the first years of CORFO is by Herman Finer, *The Chilean Development Corporation — A Study in National Planning To Raise Living Standards* (Montreal: International Labour Office, 1947). The official review of a longer period is CORFO—*Veinte años de labor 1939–1959* (Santiago, 1962).

totals in money terms might imply. If CORFO had invested deeply in the industrial activities around Santiago, we would conclude that it had increased whatever tendencies toward centralization were present in the economy. If, on the other hand, CORFO's investments were mainly rural or outside Santiago, the conclusions would be that CORFO had, consciously or not, reacted against the country's centralizing tendencies.

The records show that CORFO, whose investments are supposed to act in part as catalysts for further private investment, spent most of its money in the provinces.[21] Its most important industrial subsidiaries (*empresas filiales*) have been the National Electric Co. (ENDESA), the Pacific Steel Co. (CAP), the National Oil Co. (ENAP), and the National Sugar Co. (IANSA), all of which are outside the Santiago area. Furthermore, the current stress of CORFO on primary production (agriculture and mining) carries with it implicit encouragement for the development of the economy outside Santiago.

After 1961, CORFO's activity in regional (as opposed to central) development became even more explicit. In a series of government decrees, a set of provincial development committees was created. Their duties included reporting economic problems and investment opportunities to the central planning board of CORFO in Santiago. They were also charged with making regional studies of possible investment projects.

In addition, these provincial committees served as propaganda arms of CORFO in disseminating information about the central plan to the provinces and in trying to coordinate the private investment efforts within their particular provinces to conform with the exigencies of the plan. All these attributes of the provincial committees represented the conscious efforts by CORFO to stimulate a higher information flow between the provinces and the capital. Since the cost of this information is likely to be very low, the potential net benefits (i.e., benefits after these low costs have been subtracted) should be correspondingly high. In particular, if the goal of raising the number of alternative investment projects succeeds, and if the criteria for the allocation of investment funds are economic rather than, say, social or political, the increased flow of informa-

---

[21] "A fundamental purpose of the Program is to achieve a decentralization of production through a suitable distribution of investments, so the country might be developed harmoniously, avoiding the concentration of activities in the capital and its outskirts." CORFO, *Veinte años, op. cit.,* p. 102.

tion from the provinces will have accomplished a laudable objective. The question about the effects of centralization will also have been partially solved, since if the projects are prepared on comparable bases, it should be easy to determine whether higher returns come from investment in the center or in the provinces.

A potential danger is that the committees will turn into no more than regional lobbying groups, trying to increase their share of CORFO's limited funds at each other's expense. Insofar as the committees are able to substitute other than economic criteria for strictly economic considerations, their contribution to the economic development of the nation as a whole will be impaired.

The committees represented for CORFO another deliberate decentralization step. Eager to please everyone, even while taking this step, CORFO attacked centralism as a form of regional concentration generally antieconomic, inorganic, and politically repugnant, not in accord with the country's economic integration. At the same time, it noted that central governments, with their superior knowledge of national realities, should be the ones to make the annual decisions about the investments of social capital.[22] Presumably these two statements were not meant to be mutually contradictory: centralism can be fought while at the same time important decisions are made centrally.

The problem, of course, is that centralized concentration of decision-making power is likely to be followed by administrative and economic centralism. It would be difficult to decentralize the economic effects of decisions made centrally. Insofar as power is concentrated in one place, it will tend to attract around it at least some of the people who would be the ideal leaders in any decentralization movement. Moreover, as has been made clear, in some of the professions (medicine, teaching), students educated in the capital are often reluctant to return to their former, smaller, home towns.

Nevertheless the decentralizing tendencies of CORFO's policies seem to be very strong. Both the concentration in investments outside of Santiago and the provision of the newer regional development committees indicate an awareness of the problem of centralism and a conscious attempt at its solution.

[22] These statements were made by Alvaro Marfan, then chief of CORFO's planning and studies department in an article "Desarrollo y fomento regionales," *Industria* (monthly publication of the Sociedad de Fomento Fabril), No. 77 (September 1960), 53–59.

Conclusions

Centralization of the population in the capital city is a problem confronting many Latin American countries. Not only do the capitals seem overly large, especially to politically motivated observers from the provinces, but also their rates of population growth are higher than those of the countryside.

In Chile, the effects of this centralization are hard to measure. Employment conditions were no more favorable in Santiago than in the rest of the country. Government spending on public schools and public housing tended to further the centralization. However, the investments of the national development planning corporation (CORFO) and the creation of provincial development committees had the opposite effect.

4

The Size of the Movement
Toward Santiago

Chile's land area forms a long, narrow rectangle, about 2,600 miles long and 110 miles wide on the average. Within this territory, population density in 1960 was about 10 persons per square kilometer, as Table 4.1 shows. This table also demonstrates the dangers inherent in comparing crude population densities. If, as in the case of Chile and some other Latin American countries, the cultivable land area represents only a small percentage of the total land area, comparisons between population densities using total land area as a divisor can be completely illusory. More indicative of an economically meaningful "man/land" ratio are the data in Column 6 of the table, which show population density in the cultivable areas of selected countries. There we see that countries such as Chile, Peru, and even Brazil, which have very low crude population densities, exhibit much higher densities when we disregard the areas of the countries given over to forested lands, built-on areas, and wastelands.

The clarity of these statistics reinforce more impressionistic evidence. The map found in every Chilean schoolroom divides the country into thirds: the northern third consists of the three northern provinces of Tarapacá, Antofagasta, and Atacama, and the southern third includes Chiloé, Aisén, and Magallanes provinces. The northern third is an area of deserts and mountains, containing few elements hospitable to human life. The southern third, rainy, rocky, and forested, is similarly deserted.

Only the central third, with agricultural and forest resources to-

TABLE 4.1

POPULATION DENSITY IN SELECTED WESTERN HEMISPHERE COUNTRIES, 1960

(1) Country	(2) Population (in Thousands)	(3) Total Area (in Thousands of km²)	(4) Cultivable Area* (in Thousands of km²)	(5) Crude Population Density† (Persons/km²)	(6) Agricultural Population Density‡ (Persons/km²)	(7) Ratio of Cultivable Land to Total Land
Canada	17,909	9,976	628	2	29	6.3%
United States§	180,676	10,890	4,944	17	37	45.5
Mexico	34,988	1,973	951	18	37	48.2
Argentina	20,956	2,777	1,432	8	15	51.6
Bolivia	3,696	1,099	144	3	26	13.1
Brazil	70,600	8,512	1,610	8	44	18.9
Chile	7,627	742	137	10	56	18.5
Peru	10,857	1,235	151	9	72	12.2
Venezuela	7,331	912	192	8	38	21.1

* This figure includes both cultivated and potentially cultivable land. In particular, it includes those marginally cultivable categories of permanent meadows and pastures. Excluded are forested lands, built-on areas, and wastelands.

† Column 2 divided by Column 3.

‡ Column 2 divided by Column 4.

§ Including Alaska and Hawaii.

Sources: Table 3.1 and *FAO Production Yearbook,* Vol. 17, 1963.

gether with its Mediterranean climate, has attracted people in a substantial number. In 1960, 91.0% of Chile's people lived in the central third (more accurately, 32.0%) of its land area. This fraction of the population was roughly unchanged since the census of 1952, when 90.7% of the people lived between Coquimbo and Llanquihue provinces, which bound the central third on north and south. Details of population changes experienced during the last twenty years are shown in Table 4.2.

The Magnitude of Chilean Urban Migration

Very little interest would adhere to a phenomenon truly marginal in character. The Chilean urban migration, however, has assumed magnitudes unsymptomatic of this sort of ready adjustment to economic change.

The size of the migration can be assessed three ways. The first comes from census data. Between 1952 and 1960 the population of Chile as a whole grew at the rate of 2.7% per year. Greater Santiago during the same period grew at a much higher rate, 4.8%, while the population of the rest of the country increased only at a rate of 2.0% per year.[1] We see that the population of the Santiago metropolitan area grew at more than twice the rate of that of the rest of the country. Because Santiago's rate of natural increase (birth rate less death rate) was almost exactly equal to that of the rest of the country, any difference in total population increase must have been due to migration.[2] The generally accepted view of the

[1] These are continuously compounded growth rates. Sources include the following publications of the Dirección de Estadística y Censos and its predecessor, the Servicio Nacional de Estadística y Censos: *Algunos resultados del XIII censo de población y II de vivienda obtenidos por muestreo* (Santiago, 1962), pp. 9, 23; *Algunos resultados provinciales del II censo de vivienda obtenidos por muestreo* (Santiago, 1963), p. 1; and *XII censo general de población y I de vivienda* (Santiago, 1956), III, xviii.

[2] The following birth and death rates were calculated using 1960 population by province and 1961 births and deaths by province. All rates are per thousand population.

	Santiago Province	Non-Santiago
Birth rate	36.9	36.8
Death rate	11.2	13.0
Natural increase	25.7	23.8

Source: Dirección de Estadística, *Cifras comparativas* (Santiago, 1963), cuadro 2 and *Boletín de Estadísticas Demográficas,* Año 9, No. 2 (July 1962), 18–19.

TABLE 4.2

POPULATION DISTRIBUTION IN CHILE, 1940–1960

Region	Population (in Thousands)		
	1940	1952	1960
Three northern provinces	333.6	367.7	454.7
Nineteen central provinces	4,522.5	5,383.1	6,709.7
Three southern provinces	167.5	182.1	210.4
Total	5,023.5	5,933.0	7,375.0
	Percentage Distribution of Population		
	1940	1952	1960
Three northern provinces	6.6%	6.2%	6.2%
Nineteen central provinces	90.0	90.7	91.0
Three southern provinces	3.3	3.1	2.9
Total	100.0%	100.0%	100.0%
	Area Distribution		
	km²	Per Cent of Total Area	
Three northern provinces	258,233	34.9%	
Nineteen central provinces	235,686	31.8	
Three southern provinces	247,848	33.4	
Total	741,767	100.0%	

Sources: Servicio de Estadística y Censos, *XII censo* (1952), I, pp. 123–126, 133; Dirección de Estadística y Censos, *Algunos resultados provinciales del II censo de vivienda* (1960), p. 1.

countryside as a population spring and the city as a population sink seems to be borne out.

In addition, rural child-woman ratios (number of children aged 0–4 per thousand women aged 15–49, sometimes called a "fertility ratio") were considerably higher than the urban ones, indicating higher net rural fertility than urban.[3] Census-defined rural population grew 0.7% annually 1952–1960, while the urban population showed a 3.9% increase. Coupled with the higher rural than urban

[3] The ratio was as follows:

	1952	1960	Percentage Increase
Urban	430	543	26
Rural	696	850	22

Here, as before, urban and rural are defined according to the census definitions. "Net fertility" refers to crude birth rates less infant mortality, a measure which is approximately given by child-woman ratios. See Dirección de Estadística, *Algunos resultados del XIII censo,* cuadro 1.

child-woman ratio, migration is again indicated as the differential element.

A second way of assessing the size of the migration is the vital statistics method, possible in Chile because of the completeness with which births and deaths are registered.[4] The vital statistics method compares the natural population changes (i.e., births less deaths) by area between the 1940 and 1952 censuses with the population actually found by census enumerators in each area in those years. The difference for each area between the actual population in 1952 and that projected from natural increases during the twelve-year period is called net migration.

The censuses showed that Santiago province's population had risen from 1,286,000 in 1940 to 1,857,000 in 1952.[5] Of the net increase of 570,000, 311,000 was "natural" and 259,000 represented the net migratory movement. Thus 45% of the increase in population consisted of migrants from other provinces. The 1952 census showed that of the province's 1,755,000 enumerated people, 567,000 or 32% were natives of other provinces.

Finally, in a third method, the labor force survey of the Institute of Economics of the University of Chile verifies the continuing high proportion of migrants in the population.[6] Here, as elsewhere, "migrants" are defined simply as those not born in the area where they reside, while "natives" are defined as those born in the area where they now live. In June 1963, the survey estimated that migrants constituted 37% of the population of Greater Santiago. At the same time, of a labor force of 778,000 workers, more than half (53%) were migrants.

Each of these three methods of viewing the size of the migrant group within the general population of Santiago attests to its more-than-marginal character. We have seen that about one-third of the capital's people are migrants. Many of the children of the migrants have been born within Greater Santiago, thus making them "natives" by our definition.

A movement of this size cannot be dismissed as a marginal phe-

---

[4] Institute of Economics, *La migración interna en Chile en el período 1940–1952* (Santiago, 1959).

[5] The census figures have been adjusted upward slightly by the Institute of Economics to correct for underenumeration in the census. See preceding reference.

[6] *Ocupación y desocupación* (Santiago, quarterly since 1960). Labor force characteristics are also summarized in Institute of Economics, *La población del Gran Santiago* (Santiago, 1959).

nomenon. Instead it must be viewed as a massive adjustment involving large shifts in the population, and consequently in the work force within the country.

Geographic Origins of Santiago Migrants

Even if every person in the country outside Santiago had an equal probability of migrating to Santiago, one might reasonably expect the central third of the country to be the source of more migrants than the northern or southern thirds, since it has more people to be potential migrants. In addition, it seems clearly unreasonable to expect a resident in the far north or south, who would face far greater transportation costs, to be as likely to move to Santiago as a person in a province closer to the capital.

In 1952, 88% of the candidates for migration lived within the central third of the country and could therefore be considered within striking distance of the capital. This centralization of the population provided the setting in which the migration occurred.

The most recent statistics showing the origin of all migrants to Santiago province are found in the 1952 census.[7] As mentioned in the previous section, in 1952 1,755,000 people were counted in Santiago province, of which 567,000 (or 32.3%) were natives of other provinces. At the same time emigration from the province had occurred. There were 117,000 natives of Santiago province living in other provinces. This left a large positive balance of migration to Santiago of 450,000.

As anticipated, the bulk of the migrants came from the central third of the country. Of the 567,000 migrants, 506,000 (or 89%) were born in the eighteen other central provinces. The three northern provinces accounted for 55,000 (10%) more, while the southern provinces sent only 6,000 people to Santiago in the years before 1952.

The tendencies of the migration from the northern and southern thirds are not hard to understand within the framework of Chilean regional development characteristics. For example, railways from Santiago extend as far north as Iquique (in Tarapacá, the northernmost province), and although service is not frequent, it is at least available. On the other hand, neither public nor privately owned railway systems are present in the southern third of the country.

[7] Similar data from the 1960 census have only "third" priority among the census tasks and at this writing have not yet been tabulated.

Potential migrants can reach Santiago only by airplane or boat with rail connections.

The sources and relative rates of growth of employment possibilities seem to be even more important than transport disparities in explaining the differences in migration from far north and far south, at least between 1940 and 1952. The economic base for the three northern provinces during that period was the large copper and nitrate mines and processing plants there. For the most part owned by foreigners, they have been differentiated legally (as *gran minería*) from the smaller mines (*mediana y pequeña minería*) that were generally domestically owned.

The importance of the three northern provinces in copper and nitrate mining is shown by census data. Of 30,000 Chileans employed in copper mining, 17,000 (in 1952) lived in these provinces. Nitrate mining was even more concentrated in the north: of 27,000 employees, 26,000 were located in Tarapacá and Antofagasta provinces.[8]

Although the large nitrate *oficinas* increased their employment of blue-collar workers slightly by 9% during the intercensal period (1940–1952), this was more than offset by a 38% shrinkage of the copper work force. In all, employment in the *gran minería*, concentrated in the northern third of the country, fell by about 12%. Since employment of white-collar workers increased, blue-collar employment took the brunt of these layoffs in the large mines.

Parenthetically, labor productivity in both physical and dollar terms increased considerably over the period in the copper mines, reflecting investments in plant and equipment. At the same time, the slight increase in employment in nitrate mining and processing was mirrored by a similar increase in output, leaving labor productivity almost constant.[9]

This decrease in employment in the mines of the far north, together with its regional multiplier effects, combined to create economic pressure on the population of the area. The effects of these pressures are shown in Table 4.3. The northern provinces, although possessing 8.0% of the population outside Santiago in 1952, had sent 9.7% of Santiago's migrants to that city.

The economic situation of the southern third was different. Based

[8] *XII censo*, I, 237. Thus the large mines employed about 37% of the male work force in these three northern provinces.

[9] Institute of Economics, *Desarrollo económico de Chile 1940–1956* (Santiago, 1956), cuadros A-27, A-28, A-30, A-32, A-38, and A-40.

TABLE 4.3

CHILE: REGIONAL CONTRIBUTIONS TO MIGRATION TO SANTIAGO PROVINCE, 1952

Region	Population	Natives Living in Santiago in 1952
Three northern provinces*	367,700	54,876
Eighteen central provinces†	4,029,700	506,375
Three southern provinces‡	182,100	5,747
Total	4,579,500	566,998

	Per Cent of Chile's Population Living Outside Santiago	Per Cent of all Migrants to Santiago
Three northern provinces	8.0%	9.7%
Eighteen central provinces	88.0	89.3
Three southern provinces	4.0	1.0
Total	100.0%	100.0%

* Tarapacá, Antofagasta, and Atacama
† Excluding, of course, Santiago province
‡ Chiloé, Aisén, and Magallanes

Source: Table 4.2 and *XII censo,* III, xxvii.

at that time largely on forests, fish, and wool, its possibilities for economic expansion did not seem so limited as those of the north.[10] In addition, the south had only half the number of people to serve as potential migrants.

The combination then of differences in transport difficulties, shrinkage in mining employment, potentials for economic expansion, and differences in the population base had its effect on the number of migrants to Santiago from the far north and far south.

Most of the migrants, however, came from the central third of the country. Within this central third, the effect of distance as a discouraging factor to migration was surprisingly linear.[11] Thus the

[10] It should be noted that in the decade since 1952, iron mining and fishing in the northern provinces have acted to offset pressures brought on by declining employment in the nitrate industry.

[11] To get a number representing migrants from each province suitably corrected for differences between provinces in absolute population size, I took the following ratio for each province:

$$\frac{\text{Residents of Santiago in 1952 who were born in province } i}{\text{Population of province } i \text{ in 1940}}$$

Despite its imperfections, this ratio represented roughly the number who *did* move from each province divided by the number who *could have* moved. The nearer any given provincial capital was to Santiago, the more likely we were to find large blocks of natives from that province in Santiago.

If we cast Chilean migration in the crude framework of the "push" and "pull" hypotheses outlined in Chapter 2, I would favor the "pull" for the central third, the "push" for the northern third, and would call the migration from the southern third negligible. The factors creating economic pressures in the north, especially in the mines, support the "push" hypothesis for that region.

At the same time, in the central provinces the observed decrease in the relative number of migrants as distance increased made the pull hypothesis more attractive. We have seen a negatively sloped straight-line relationship between distance from Santiago and relative number of migrants to Santiago. Given increasing transport costs with increasing distances as a barrier to be overcome, only a rural poverty more or less uniform over the whole central third could be consistent with this observation *and* with the push hypothesis. The varying conditions of soil, terrain, rainfall, land tenure, and economic opportunities in nearby towns make a uniform rural poverty seem unlikely. But if rural poverty varied from one area to another, and further, if it really affected the number of people who migrated as the push suggests, then this relative number of migrants would not have varied so uniformly with distance, but would have formed a more unorganized scatter when plotted against distance. The linearity which in fact resulted seems to indicate that the pull was more forceful than the push.

At the same time, as observed earlier, rigidly separating these two hypotheses obscures their essential complementarity. If we insist on viewing migration as an economic phenomenon — a view which sometimes seems forced — then it seems likely that each decision to move results from some combination of push and pull.

Migrant Origins – Urban or Rural

The migrants' residence histories hold the key for some important economic conclusions. Many patterns are possible. The rural resident could come directly to Santiago. On the other hand, he could

---

correlation between this ratio and distance by rail from the provincial capitals to Santiago was $r^2 = 0.78$. Visual inspection of a scatter diagram showing distance and the ratio indicates that the fit was better for the southern provinces (within the central third) than for the provinces nearer to Santiago.

come to the capital at the end of a series of moves which had taken him first from the farm to a neighboring small town and then to cities of ever-increasing size until finally he reached the biggest one. In a third possible pattern, the resident of a large town could move to Santiago, his place being taken by the former resident of a still smaller town, and so on, until at the end of the chain, the peasant left the land and moved to some nearby small town. This, of course, describes the pattern found by Ravenstein and Redford in nine-teenth-century England.[12]

Our conclusions about the migrants will be affected by the residential history pattern uncovered. Direct moves from the country-side to the city upset existing cultural patterns most. Typically, peasants are illiterate and unskilled. They lack exposure to the money economy, since most transactions are in kind on the *fundos* from which they come. Women generally do not compete with men in the rural labor market, nor are they a source of money income for the family.

In contrast, in the city nearly everyone is literate. Skills are more widely distributed among the working population. Although payments in kind remain, they have shrunk to a fraction of the total income of the urban worker. Men and women are often interchangeable in office and commercial positions, and the female participation rate in the urban labor force is about two and one-half times the rural rate.[13]

The effects of these cultural differences on the migrant will be less disrupting if he has lived in a series of towns before coming to the capital, thus becoming accustomed to urban living and working conditions. And clearly the necessary workers' adjustments are smallest when city dwellers move to bigger cities while farmers go to small towns, as in the Ravenstein-Redford case.

Apparently the pattern of English internal migration experienced during the Industrial Revolution has been repeated in Chile. Two pieces of evidence support this conclusion.

The first compares the responses given in two sample surveys made in Greater Santiago.[14] To an employment survey of the Institute of Economics, 63% of the migrants replied that they had been

---

[12] Chapter 2 contains details of their findings.

[13] Part of the lower rural participation rate for women is a definitional matter, since farm wives are excluded from the labor force.

[14] Technical descriptions of the surveys mentioned in this paragraph and the next one are found in Appendices A and B.

born in towns later identified as having more than 10,000 people in 1952. In a separate survey, the Latin American Demographic Center questioned migrants on their residential histories. Although the results of this survey have not been completely tabulated, preliminary findings show that 65% lived in towns of more than 5,000 immediately before coming to Santiago. If we had observed a pattern of migrants with repeated moves from smaller towns to larger, the percentage *born in towns* would have to be far smaller than the percentage *living in towns* immediately before coming to Santiago. Since these percentages were in fact similar, the data are consistent with the Ravenstein-Redford hypothesis on movement.

The second piece of evidence comes from a sample survey of economically active recent migrants. Taking note of criticisms of the earlier employment survey of the Institute of Economics, this inquest carefully asked for residential histories.[15] When respondents replied, for instance, that they were born outside Santiago in a large town, the interviewer always asked, "In that town itself, or in the country outside it?" In this way, the accuracy of the responses was perhaps more assured than in the original employment survey, where it was feared that the town nearest the birthplace might often have been named as the birthplace itself.

The results of the survey of economically active recent migrants were surprisingly similar to the earlier surveys, which had covered all migrants. Two-thirds of the economically active migrants had been born in towns of more than 10,000 (1960 census). Only about one-seventh claimed places of birth with fewer than 1,000 inhabitants — places which could be classified as clearly rural. The contrast between the distribution of population by size of city and the distribution of the recent migrants by size of birthplace is shown in the following table.[16]

---

[15] Some objections, probably justified, had been registered against the use of place-of-birth data from the Institute's employment survey. The respondents were asked for their *lugar de nacimiento* (place of birth). Some observers, skeptical of the quality of the answers, have said that respondents would tend to give the name of the nearest big town to their birthplace or that the interviewer would tend to repeat the question until the respondent named a town of sufficient size to be familiar to him. To the extent that this occurred, it would naturally bias the results, making migrants' origins seem more urban than they really were.

[16] The population distribution column in this table comes from data in Dirección de Estadística y Censos, *Cifras provisorias del número de habitantes y de viviendas según censo de población de 1960* (Santiago, 1963; mimeographed).

City Size (1960)	Distribution of Population Outside Santiago	Distribution of Migrant Birthplaces
More than 100,000 (excluding Santiago)	9.4%	9.4%
50,000–100,000	10.4	20.0
20,000–50,000	13.1	16.5
10,000–20,000	6.1	14.2
Less than 10,000	60.9	33.8
Foreign born	—	6.1
Total population (excluding Santiago)	100.0%	100.0%

Thus far, we have established only one-half of the Ravenstein-Redford migration pattern, viz., that the migrants to the biggest city came largely from smaller cities rather than from the countryside. That their places in the towns were filled by former rural residents can fortunately be deduced from census data on population and from the industrial distribution of the people who were economically active.

Preliminary results of the 1960 census showed that none of the 59 cities with more than 10,000 people had undergone a decline in population between the 1952 and 1960 censuses.[17] Some of the cities smaller than Santiago experienced dramatic population growth. At the same time that census-defined urban population was growing at the annual rate of 3.9%, the rural population increased only by 0.7% per year (1952–1960). Too, the economically active population engaged in agriculture rose only from 629,000 in 1952 to 648,000 in 1960, an increase of but 0.4% per year.[18] Migration was plainly stripping people from the agricultural parts of the country. We have already seen that these rural people, in general, were not those found in Santiago. They must therefore have gone to the smaller towns.

I have tried here to establish that the Ravenstein-Redford migration patterns were seen in Chile: that the migration formed a series of stages or waves, in which people from the towns went to the cities and people from the rural districts went into the towns.[19] The

[17] Ibid.

[18] These data are derived from figures given in *Cifras comparativas de los censos de 1940 y 1952 y muestra del censo de 1960* (Santiago: Dirección de Estadística y Censos, 1963).

[19] Some evidence suggests that postwar internal migration in West Germany followed the same patterns. See Karl Schwarz, "Migration in the Federal Re-

economic effects of this movement are still to be ascertained, but the establishment of the pattern is an important first step in uncovering these effects.

Length of Residence in Santiago

Just as alternative patterns in residential history suggest conclusions to the economist, so also does the time pattern of the movement. Frenetic short-term movements, frequently reversing themselves, imply different conclusions from a smoothly flowing long-term, one-way migration. The data covering the Santiago migration indicate that the latter pattern predominates.

The length of residence of the migrants discovered by the labor force survey of the Institute of Economics shows that movement to the city has not fluctuated significantly during the past five years. Table 4.4 also indicates that almost three-fifths of the migrants have lived in Santiago for more than ten years, thus giving a settled permanence to the group of migrants considered as a whole. The slight bulge in migrants with three years of residence can be traced to the occurrence of severe earthquakes in Chile's south three years before the survey was taken.

The comparative absence of return movement was demonstrated by data in the survey of economically active recent migrants. Of these migrants, all of whom had moved to Santiago within the last ten years, only one-seventh knew anyone who had come to Santiago to live and who had subsequently returned to his place of origin for any reason.[20] This type of permanence contrasts strikingly with conditions in Africa, where nearly all migrants go back to their former homes after a period of a few years in industrial employment.[21]

In Chile this combination of an even flow, not varying widely

public of Germany by Town and County," *Proceedings of the International Population Conference*, 1961, Vol. 4, Paper No. 97.

[20] In reading an early draft of this manuscript, Paul Schultz noted that the same results would also come from an inflow tapering off over the years, coupled with a substantial return flow. He remarked that "asking about returnees is suggestive but inconclusive evidence." I agree.

[21] Articles exploring the economic and cultural explanations for African migration include Walter Elkan, "Migrant Labor in Africa: An Economist's Approach," *American Economic Review*, Vol. 49, No. 2 (May 1959), 188–197; and J. Van Velsen, "Labor Migration as a Positive Factor in the Continuity of Tonga Tribal Society," *Economic Development and Cultural Change*, Vol. 8, No. 3 (April 1960), 265–278.

from year to year, together with a lack of massive return migration, gives an additional cast of stability to the migratory process. Combined with the gradual nature of the urbanization of the migrants

TABLE 4.4

SANTIAGO, CHILE: LENGTH OF RESIDENCE FOR MIGRANTS

Length of Residence (in Years)	Percentage of Migrants with Indicated Length of Residence
0	4.8%
1	4.1
2	3.6
3	4.5
4	3.5
5	3.3
6–10	16.0
11 or more	59.8
No data	0.3
Total	100.0%

Source: Institute of Economics, unpublished data from employment survey for June 1963.

shown in the previous section, the picture emerges of migration as a process that does not provide strain for the society in the same way that African and Indian migrations have.

Summary

This chapter has tried to establish that internal migration and particularly migration to Santiago have been more than marginal phenomena influencing population distribution within Chile. Unlike internal migrants in some of the least developed countries, the Chilean migrants have proceeded to Santiago mostly from cities and towns instead of coming directly from agricultural districts. Connected with a lack of rural ties is the suggestion by the data that return or back-and-forth migration is uncommon.

5

Patterns of Labor Supply

Chilean patterns of employment and unemployment provide valuable suggestions about the intensity of use of labor resources within the economy. This chapter treats unemployment in the nation as a whole and in Santiago, trying to evaluate the relevance for Chile of the following plausible hypotheses:

(1) In a developing country, change most obviously manifests itself in industrialization. It is hypothesized that industrialization and urbanization go hand in hand, owing (*a*) to the attractions which urban industrial job opportunities have on would-be migrants and (*b*) to the external economies for industrial enterprises provided by a large urban labor market and the availability of urban social overhead capital.

(2) When the over-all rate of urban unemployment rises, it is commonly assumed that the first workers to become unemployed are those in manufacturing and construction. As a result, relative employment (the proportion of the labor force employed) in the easier-to-enter commerce and service trades becomes larger. With a *declining* rate of over-all unemployment, the opposite effect will be seen.

(3) Migration to a specific urban center depends largely on job opportunities there. The unemployment rate in the city measures the presence of these opportunities. Very tight labor markets indicate that labor demand outstrips supply at the current wage rate; massive unemployment shows the absence of opportunities relative to the number of potential workers, again, given the level and structure of wage rates. One widespread belief is that lower rates of unemployment will draw more migrants to a city.

Relationships between industrialization, urbanization, and migration are clearly central to the development process. Although empirical observations for one country will not prove hypotheses, they may well provide counter-examples for erroneous or overly broad generalizations made in the past.

Chilean Unemployment in 1960

Unemployment in Santiago was somewhat higher than in the rest of the country at the census date in 1960.[1] Comparing the over-all rates for Santiago (8.3%) and the rest of the country (6.7%), however, is not too meaningful an exercise. The demographic and economic threads that finally culminate in an aggregate such as an unemployment rate are long and deviously tangled. Only by unraveling them may we hope to understand them.

For the higher Santiago unemployment rate, some "explanations" suggest themselves immediately. Some, however, can be shown to be false upon the most elementary disaggregation of the data. It might be said, for example, that women were more active and therefore more unemployed in the Santiago labor market than outside Santiago. Without question Santiago women were more active. While 31.0% of them worked or sought work, only 18.7% of their counterparts outside Santiago followed their example.[2] The census figures in Table 5.1 show that both in Santiago *and* in the rest of the country, 4.6% of the women in the labor force were unemployed, despite the disparity in participation rates. Thus the greater female activity in the capital did not explain the higher over-all unemployment rate there.

Another possible approach would be to explain the difference in Santiago and non-Santiago unemployment rates by the differences in the age compositions of the two groups. In Santiago, it might be claimed, more people fell within the age groups in which the incidence of unemployment is highest. Table 5.2 shows that in the mid-range age groups (20–44), Santiago had relatively more people and a higher unemployment percentage. On the other hand, in the

[1] *Algunos resultados del XIII censo de población y II de vivienda* (Santiago: Dirección de Estadística y Censos, 1963), and unpublished data of the Dirección de Estadística y Censos.

[2] Only women in the potentially working ages, here defined as fifteen and over, are included in these participation rates. Farm wives are definitionally excluded from the labor force. See also pp. 76–77n.

TABLE 5.1
CHILE: UNEMPLOYMENT, 1960, BY SEX

	Economically Active (in Thousands)	Number of Unemployed (in Thousands)			Unemployment Rate		
		Previously Employed	First-time Work Seekers	Total	Previously Employed	First-time Work Seekers	Total
Whole Country							
Total	2,356.0	117.6	49.9	167.5	5.0%	2.1%	7.1%
Men	1,837.8	103.7	40.2	143.9	5.6	2.2	7.8
Women	518.2	13.9	9.7	23.6	2.7	1.9	4.6
Santiago							
Total	665.2	42.2	12.7	54.9	6.3	1.9	8.3
Men	443.3	35.7	9.1	44.8	8.1	2.1	10.1
Women	221.9	6.5	3.6	10.1	2.9	1.6	4.6
Outside Santiago							
Total	1,690.8	75.4	37.2	112.6	4.5	2.2	6.7
Men	1,394.5	68.0	31.1	99.1	4.9	2.2	7.1
Women	296.3	7.4	6.1	13.5	2.5	2.1	4.6

Source: Algunos resultados del XIII censo de población y II de vivienda (Santiago, Dirección de Estadística y Censos, 1962) and unpublished data from the Dirección de Estadística y Censos.

TABLE 5.2

CHILE: AGE DISTRIBUTION OF THE WORKING AGE POPULATION AND
UNEMPLOYMENT BY AGE GROUP

Age Group	Santiago		Outside Santiago		Total	
	Age Distribution	Per Cent Unemployed	Age Distribution	Per Cent Unemployed	Age Distribution	Per Cent Unemployed
15–19	15.1%	19.4%	16.9%	15.5%	16.4%	16.4%
20–29	25.9	8.8	25.0	6.6	25.3	7.2
30–44	30.4	4.8	27.5	4.7	28.3	4.7
45–64	22.3	7.2	23.1	4.2	22.9	5.0
65+	6.3	8.3	7.4	4.9	7.1	5.5
Total	100.0%	8.3%	100.0%	6.7%	100.0%	7.1%

Source: Algunos resultados del XIII censo de población y II de vivienda (Santiago, Dirección de Estadística y Censos, 1962) and unpublished data from the Dirección de Estadística y Censos.

TABLE 5.3
CHILE: UNEMPLOYMENT, 1960, BY AGE

	Economically Active (in Thousands)	Number of Unemployed (in Thousands)			Unemployment Rate		
		Previously Employed	First-time Work Seekers	Total	Previously Employed	First-time Work Seekers	Total
Whole Country							
15–19	316.2	15.2	36.7	51.9	4.8%	11.6%	16.4%
20–29	686.1	37.4	12.3	49.7	5.4	1.8	7.2
30–44	744.3	34.1	0.9	35.0	4.6	0.1	4.7
45–64	524.2	26.2	—	26.2	5.0	—	5.0
65+	85.2	4.7	—	4.7	5.5	—	5.5
Santiago							
15–19	74.9	5.5	9.0	14.5	7.3%	12.0%	19.4%
20–29	203.6	14.6	3.4	18.0	7.2	1.7	8.8
30–44	231.7	10.8	0.3	11.1	4.7	0.1	4.8
45–64	139.3	10.0	—	10.0	7.2	—	7.2
65+	15.7	1.3	—	1.3	8.3	—	8.3
Outside Santiago							
15–19	241.3	9.7	27.7	37.4	4.0%	11.5%	15.5%
20–29	482.5	22.8	8.9	31.7	4.7	1.8	6.6
30–44	512.6	23.3	0.6	23.9	4.5	0.1	4.7
45–64	384.9	16.2	—	16.2	4.2	—	4.2
65+	69.5	3.4	—	3.4	4.9	—	4.9

Source: Same as for Table 5.1.

oldest and youngest age groups (below twenty and above forty-four), Santiago once again had relatively more unemployment (i.e., a higher unemployment rate), but fewer people. Thus the explanation using the distinct age compositions of Santiago and the rest of the country to explain unemployment has only limited value.

Some light may be shed on the problem by the comparison of *types* of unemployment by sex. Two types of unemployed people are considered here: those seeking work for the first time and those who have previously held jobs and are seeking work again (*cesantes*). These two types might be characterized as new workers and experienced unemployed. The only significant differences between Santiago and the rest of the country were for men who had previously held jobs. The Santiaguinos in this class were more prone to unemployment (8.1%) than were the non-Santiago residents (4.9%). In contrast, women in both classes and men seeking work for the first time did not exhibit substantial differences in measured unemployment.

The data on age distribution of unemployment give this evidence added weight. They show (Table 5.3) that unemployment of previously employed people in Santiago fluctuated widely between the different age groups (going from 4.7% to 8.3%). Comparable figures for the non-Santiago population show a surprising uniformity, extending only from 4.0% to 4.9%.

These variations in the patterns of unemployment between Santiago and the rest of Chile can probably be explained by the differences in the industrial (or occupational) distribution of the labor force. The predominant occupation outside the capital is farming; about three of every eight non-Santiago members of the labor force are farmers. Male employment is clearly more important than female employment in agriculture.[3] Furthermore, agriculture as an occupation is easy to enter and to re-enter, if need be, after the loss of another job. Unemployment rates for males of all ages outside Santiago are therefore lower than those for Santiago men.

Occupational and Industrial Distribution of the Labor Force

If Chile were a developing country at the most primitive level, the now familiar "dual" economy might exist there. The differences between Santiago and the rest of the country would then be re-

---

[3] Of course, census definitions which exclude farm wives from the labor force affect this result.

flected by an urban, cosmopolitan, industrial capital contrasting with a rural, backward, primarily agricultural hinterland. The resultant occupational and industrial distribution of the labor force would show these differences. The capital city would have the bulk of its people in manufacturing and specialized services such as finance, government, and real estate, while in the rest of the country, in addition to agriculture itself, transportation and trade would predominate, manufacturing being almost wholly absent.

This hypothetical picture of Chile exaggerates, of course, and the degree of economic development outside Santiago is the chief victim of this distortion. Tables 5.4 and 5.5 show the industrial and occupational distributions of the Chilean labor force in 1960. In calculating the percentage distributions, I have excluded agriculture and mining, since almost all these activities are carried on outside Santiago. After this exclusion has been made, the similarity

TABLE 5.4
CHILE: OCCUPATIONAL DISTRIBUTION OF THE LABOR FORCE, 1960

| Occupational Group | Numbers (in Thousands) | | | Percentages* | |
	Santiago	Outside Santiago	Chile	Santiago	Outside Santiago
Professionals and technicians	50.4	70.9	121.3	7.8%	6.9%
Managers	17.1	23.8	40.9	2.6	2.3
Office workers	83.2	78.7	161.9	12.9	7.7
Salesmen	66.6	97.8	164.4	10.3	9.6
Farmers and fishermen	17.7	614.4	632.1	—	—
Miners and quarrymen	1.8	55.5	57.3	—	—
Drivers	23.8	53.9	77.7	3.7	5.3
Artisans and operatives	206.2	318.3	524.5	31.9	31.2
Manual workers	33.5	85.8	119.3	5.2	8.4
Personal service workers	122.7	179.1	301.8	19.0	17.5
Others	42.2	112.6	154.8	6.5	11.0
Total	665.2	1,690.8	2,356.0		
Total, excluding farmers and miners	645.7	1,020.9	1666.6	100.0%	100.0%

* Excluding agriculture and mining.

Source: Algunos resultados del XIII censo de población y II de vivienda (Santiago: Dirección de Estadística y Censos, 1962) and unpublished data from the Dirección de Estadística y Censos.

TABLE 5.5
CHILE: INDUSTRIAL DISTRIBUTION OF THE LABOR FORCE, 1960

Industrial Group	Numbers (in Thousands)			Percentages*	
	Santiago	Outside Santiago	Chile	Santiago	Outside Santiago
Agriculture and fishing	15.0	633.0	648.0	—	—
Mining	3.8	93.5	97.3	—	—
Manufacturing	187.2	218.8	406.0	28.9%	22.7%
Construction	55.0	109.5	164.5	8.5	11.4
All services	225.9	342.5	568.4	34.9	35.5
Commerce	98.7	126.6	225.3	15.3	13.1
Transport and communications	35.0	85.2	120.2	5.4	8.8
Unspecified activities	44.6	81.7	126.3	6.9	8.5
Total	665.2	1,690.8	2,356.0		
Total, excluding agriculture and mining	646.4	964.3	1,610.7	100.0%	100.0%

* Excluding agriculture and mining.

Source: *Algunos resultados del XIII censo de población y II de vivienda* (Santiago: Dirección de Estadística y Censos, 1962) and unpublished data from the Dirección de Estadística y Censos.

between the patterns of labor use in Santiago and the rest of the country are somewhat surprising. To be sure, there are relatively more highly skilled white-collar jobs in Santiago (33.6% of the labor force) than outside (26.5%). Too, the number of drivers and un-skilled manual workers in the rest of Chile (13.7%) surpasses that of the capital (8.9%).

But almost exactly the same proportions of the population outside agriculture work as artisans and operatives. And practically one-fourth of those outside Santiago are employed in manufacturing (22.7%), while the capital's manufacturing workers do not occupy a startlingly more important place as a part of the work force (28.9%). Furthermore, commerce in the rest of the country, even after agriculture has been excluded, is a less important employer than it is in Santiago.

These comparisons clarify the picture of the labor force in Santiago and outside it. Within Santiago, industrialization has not ad-vanced too far, compared with the continued strength of more traditional tertiary activities. At the same time, outside Santiago, agriculture employs only three-eighths of the (non-Santiago) labor force. In addition there is more manufacturing and less economic activity directly ancillary to agriculture than we might have expected from the overdrawn portrait which began this section.

Trends in Unemployment

The stagnation of Chilean national income during the 1950's was accompanied by increasing unemployment. Over-all unemployment rates rose from 3.6% of the work force in 1952 to 7.1% in 1960. Once again, previously employed men were more likely to be affected by this increase than men seeking work for the first time or than women in either category. The average annual growth rates of numbers of people unemployed in these classes is shown in the following table:[4]

Chile: Growth Rates of the Unemployed Labor Force, 1952–1960

	Men	Women
New workers	5.6%	4.6%
Experienced unemployed	12.4%	6.6%

Thus we see that men, virtually forced to remain in the labor market in order to support their families, suffered greater increases in unemployment than did women, most of whom presumably had the option to leave the work force in the face of weak demand for labor.[5]

The suspicion lurks, however, that the two points represented by the census dates do not represent the true trend of unemployment. The revival of the economy during 1961 and 1962 alters our less than cheerful view of the economic situation. Over-all unemployment for Greater Santiago fell from its highest point of more than 10% in March 1959 to a low of 4.3% in September 1962, and has since stabilized at a level of somewhat more than 5%.[6] If these data on

[4] For example, the number of men out of work who were previously employed rose from 38,400 in 1952 to 103,700 in 1960. Thus their numbers grew by 12.4% per year; as with all growth rates in this book, this rate is an average annual rate, continuously compounded.

[5] U.S. experience with changes in participation rates resulting from changes in aggregate demand are well documented in William G. Bowen and T. A. Finegan, "Labor Force Participation and Unemployment," in Arthur M. Ross, ed., *Employment Policy and the Labor Market* (Berkeley and Los Angeles: University of California Press, 1965), pp. 115–161, and Kenneth Strand and Thomas Dernberg, "Cyclical Variation in Labor Force Participation," *Review of Economics and Statistics*, Vol. 46, No. 4 (November 1964), 378–391.

[6] The data in this paragraph were drawn from the employment sample survey for Greater Santiago of the Institute of Economics of the University of Chile. The most recent period included in the analysis is the third quarter of 1963.

the level of unemployment may be generalized to the economy as a whole, they indicate that the 1960 census date nearly coincided with unemployment's peak level.

In addition to the problem of having only two points from the census on which to base our ideas of a "trend," there is also the problem of the relation between the measurement of unemployment for Greater Santiago and the comparable measure for Chile as a whole. The following table compares types of unemployment for April 1960 as a percentage of the labor force:

Chile: Unemployment, April 1960

Type of Unemployment	Greater Santiago		Chile
	Census	Survey	Census
New workers	1.9%	1.1%	2.1%
Experienced unemployed	6.3	6.3	5.0
Total	8.3%	7.3%	7.1%

Unfortunately, no systematic differences emerge from this comparison. Census data for Santiago show relatively more first-time work seekers, but the same proportion of older members of the labor force who were looking for work. Both sets of data for Santiago reinforce our previously stated idea that urban unemployment, especially among those who have formerly held jobs, was higher than unemployment in the rest of the country. Generalizing Santiago unemployment figures to represent unemployment in the country as a whole must therefore be done with some caution.

Unemployment Patterns and the Distribution of the Labor Force

A number of hypotheses try to link the over-all rate of unemployment, representing the slack in the economy at given wage rates, with the patterns of employment in the various economic sectors. In the most common of these hypotheses, the unemployment rate varies inversely with the relative number employed in manufacturing or in the "secondary" sector of the economy (say, manufacturing and construction). Employment in manufacturing is the first to feel the effects of an economic downturn, says the hypothesis. Orders dwindle, inventories pile up, and operatives are laid off. They drift into the services, especially nonprofessional and personal services, and into petty commerce, where self-employment and nonpaid family employment are more prevalent, skill levels are lower, and

entry is easier than in the goods sector. In order to be fully opera-
tive, of course, the hypothesis specifies the opposite behavior in the
case of an economic upturn: the ranks of the services shrink as
workers leave for more remunerative wage-work in goods.

This hypothesis was contradicted by employment experience in
Santiago. As shown in Figure 5.1, employment in secondary activities

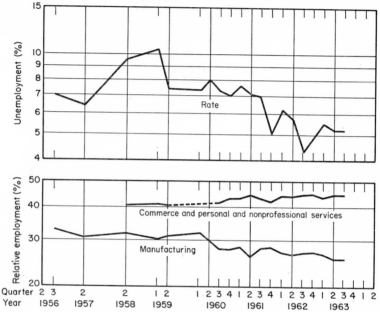

FIGURE 5.1.   *Chile: A comparison of over-all unemployment with the
percentage of the labor force employed in various branches of
economic activity. (Data refer to Greater Santiago only.)*

Source: Institute of Economics employment survey data for Greater Santiago.

— manufacturing and construction — was *positively* correlated with
the level of unemployment.[7] Employment in personal services and
in the aggregate of commerce, personal services, and nonprofessional services was negatively related with the global unemployment rate, instead of positively related as the hypothesis suggests.[8]

If a seemingly logical hypothesis regarding the employment be-

---

[7] The positive correlation is not strong, but it at least is not negative:
$r^2 = 0.29$ for the correlation between relative employment in manufacturing
(percentage of the employed labor force working in manufacturing) and the
over-all unemployment rate. A similar correlation using manufacturing and construction instead of manufacturing alone gives an r^2 of 0.31. Both coefficients
are significant at the 5% level but not at the 1% level.

havior of part of an economy has been shown to be false, we should seek another, more consistent, hypothesis. A simple reversal of the causal mechanism in the rejected hypothesis accomplishes the task. The new hypothesis specifies that higher employment in the services, where entry is easier and self-employment more prevalent, is reflected in lower over-all unemployment rates. The over-all unemployment rate can be considered as a weighted average of the unemployment rates in the various economic sectors. The services have a measured rate of unemployment lower than the goods industries, as shown for a typical period by the following table:[9]

Greater Santiago: Unemployment Rates by Branch of Activity, June 1960

Manufacturing	8.3%
Construction	16.3
Commerce	4.5
Transportation	7.1
Government and financial services	4.4
Personal and other services	4.8
Over-all unemployment	8.0%

In an economic stagnation, when investment activity is notable by its absence, the swelling of the services as important employers of manpower reflects the low investment necessary for the initiation of most of these activities. Neither complex physical plants nor prolonged periods of education and training need be undertaken in many of the service and commerce occupations. The consequent ease of entry into these branches with their resulting low degree of unemployment seems thus to have weighted the over-all unemployment rate in a downward direction.

The trend toward services, or at least away from production of goods, is also present at the national level. Employment in the goods-producing industries, including agriculture and mining, dropped

[8] These (negative) correlations between service employment and over-all unemployment are stronger than the ones cited in note 7 for manufacturing. Between personal services and unemployment, for example, the r^2 is 0.653, while for the combination of commerce, personal services, and nonprofessional services, we get an r^2 of 0.606. Both of these coefficients are significant at the 1% level.

[9] *Ocupación y desocupación, septiembre de 1963, op. cit.,* p. 30. Data for any other date would have shown approximately the same variation in unemployment in the various branches of the economy.

from 58.4% of the labor force in 1952 to 55.8% in 1960, according to the census. The drop in goods employment was especially pronounced among the women, where the proportion employed in goods fell from 33.0% to 24.7%.

At both the national and local levels, we might characterize the service sector as a residual employer. The absolute number of people employed in goods production remained almost constant. The labor force, on the other hand, increased in size. The new entrants to the labor force seem to have drifted into the services.[10]

Some numbers dramatize this concept. Between 1952 and 1960, the Chilean labor force at work or looking for work in manufacturing remained almost constant, rising only from 405,100 to 406,000. Mining fell from 101,000 to 97,300. Agriculture rose only marginally from 629,000 to 648,000. Within the primary and secondary sectors of the economy, only construction, employing largely unskilled workers, showed any dynamism between the census dates, rising from 101,800 to 164,500. This rise would augur better for the future were it not for construction's notorious economic instability, an instability which makes itself felt in the number employed with only a very short lag.

Within Greater Santiago between 1960 and 1963 these trends were felt with even greater force. While numbers employed in manufacturing were rising by 1,900 and in construction by 2,600, branches such as commerce were using 21,200 more workers and the personal and other services rose as employers by 30,800.[11] With a concurrent labor force increase of 70,800, it seems fairly clear that employment in the goods-producing industries was almost constant, leaving the services as the residual employers of the increases in the labor force.

[10] In much the same vein, G. C. Allen views the growth of the tertiary sector in Japan between 1914 and 1930. Instead of representing the growth of economic prosperity, as the well-known Colin Clark thesis suggests, the services grew in Japan because "opportunities for employment in the new capital-intensive industries were insufficient to provide occupation for the large annual additions to the labor force. Much of the increase in this period, therefore, found its way into the small-scale industries or the service trades where productivity was low. Striking contrasts between the incomes of those employed in the modern sector of the economy and the small-scale sector appeared." *A Short Economic History of Modern Japan,* second revised edition (London: Unwin University Books, 1962), p. 125.

[11] *Ocupación y desocupación, op. cit.,* September 1963, p. 26. The changes in employment given in this paragraph are changes between the average employment in each sector during the last three quarters of 1960 and the first three quarters of 1963.

The stagnation of the economy thus provided a situation of employment by economic sectors different than the one postulated at the beginning of this chapter. Increasing urbanization seems to have been unaccompanied by a proportional increase in industrialization.

Unemployment and Migration

The third theme to be touched on in this chapter is the relation between unemployment within Greater Santiago and migration. The presence of job opportunities, presumably signaled by a tight labor market and characterized by a low level of unemployment, is customarily assumed to attract migrants to an area, while a high rate of unemployment reflecting economic malaise is said to repel migration.

Despite the plausibility of these hypotheses, the migration to Santiago does not seem to have been a function of the rate of unemployment within the capital. Table 4.4, for instance, showed that the year-by-year entrance into the city by migrants from 1958 to 1963 did not vary substantially.[12] The same pattern presented itself for the years in the mid-fifties.[13] This steady flow of migrants was observed despite the changes in measured unemployment in Greater Santiago, which rose from 7% in October 1956 to more than 10% in September 1959 and fell to about 5% during 1963.

The failure of the hypothesis linking migration and unemployment can be explained in two ways. The first and most obvious explanation is that the *hypothesis* is false. In other words, urban migration was not responsive to shifts of the observed magnitude in the unemployment rate. People continued to pour into the city despite the fluctuations in the state of the labor market.

An alternative explanation would claim that in a very real sense *the data themselves* were false. It might be said, for example, that migration was indeed responsive to changes in the *real* unemployment rate, the problem being that the *measured* rate of unemployment was not an adequate indication of the real rate. We have seen already in this chapter that a drop in the measured over-all rate of unemployment coincided with an increase in the importance of

---

[12] Allowing, as we did in Chapter 4, for small amounts of mortality among the migrants and for a small quantity of return migration in every year.

[13] Data on length of residence have been extracted from unpublished figures in the labor force survey of the Institute of Economics. Two surveys were used: June 1958 and June 1963.

services as a source of employment. It seems almost beyond question that underemployment or disguised unemployment is more prevalent within the services than in the goods-producing part of the economy. If this degree of greater underemployment in the services could be translated into some equivalent rate of unemployment, it is possible that the rate of unemployment thus calculated did not change during the period under observation. This uniformity in the real rate of unemployment coupled with a uniformity in the flow of migration to Santiago at least would not contradict the hypothesis as stated: that migration rates varied with varying unemployment rates.

However interesting it may be to speculate on this question, the data do not permit us to decide between these rival explanations. Notably absent are data which would allow the calculation of the equivalent amount of unemployment present in underemployment in the services.

The appeal of both explanations is strong, however, and I should like to attempt to combine what I feel to be the most attractive features of both. For instance, from the first explanation, the relative insensitivity of migrants to what may appear to them to be marginal economic changes has already been asserted.[14] In addition, it seems clear that changes in measured unemployment acquire a bias when services gain as employers. As this shift toward the services continues, "real" unemployment, at least as a concept, becomes progressively higher than measured unemployment.

Conclusions

What may we salvage from the three statements made at the beginning of this chapter? Not much, it appears. Industrialization, at least in its effects on employment, proceeded very slowly, and was almost as far advanced outside Santiago as within the capital. Falling unemployment rates within Santiago were associated with a shift to the services as relatively more important employers of the labor force. Finally, there seemed to be little variation in migration to Santiago accompanying the fluctuations in the measured rate of unemployment there.

[14] In Chapter 2.

6

Migration Selectivity

The effects of migration depend in part on the nature of the migrant, the people he leaves behind him, and the group into which he comes. Demographers call migration "selective" in the sense that the migrants do not represent a random sample of the population. This selectivity can be defined either in terms of the population groups from which the migrants come or in terms of those they join at their destination. In this chapter, I will try to make both comparisons whenever possible.

Broad generalizations about the selectivity of migration are easy to find. Donald J. Bogue has written:[1]

> It is widely appreciated that migration is highly selective of younger persons. This arises because each oncoming generation must adapt to the social and economic changes that are taking place. This is the price neophytes must pay to get an acceptable and secure socio-economic "niche" in the social organization. Where these changes require a shift of population, it is the younger, more flexible, and less burdened members who re-examine the distributional imbalance and make the needed movements. As a corollary of this, if marital status is determined before migration, it is found that migrants tend to be single, widowed, or divorced persons rather than married.

He goes on to generalize, "As yet demographers have not succeeded

[1] "Techniques and Hypotheses for the Study of Differential Migration: Some Notes from an Experiment with U.S. Data," *Proceedings of the International Population Conference*, 1961, Vol. 2, Session 4, Paper No. 114. Emphasis in original.

in establishing any other 'universal' migration differential." He later concludes, *"Further universal migration differentials do not exist and should not be expected to exist."* Why should they not be expected? Because "Migration is a concomitant of social change, and migration selectivity fluctuates with the nature of social change and the composition of the population that is involved in the change."

Thus Bogue suggests that the migration differentials are, in effect, responses to stimuli that vary from country to country and over time within a given country. In this chapter we will be interested not so much in the stimuli that cause the migration differentials as in the effects of the differential responses from the population. For our purposes, the population may be divided into groups by age, sex, education, occupation, and other characteristics. Standardizing within any one of these classifications, we will then look at the differences between migrants and the rest of the population.

This standardization is essential if we want to distinguish differences between migrants and other people — differences that are in some sense *real,* stemming from innate differences (if any exist) between those who move and those who do not. The migrants, for instance, may be older or younger than the rest of the population, may contain a greater or smaller proportion of women, and may consist of people with widely differing occupations. To compare migrants and natives *without* standardizing, and then to attribute differences found to inherent differences between the two groups, would be like comparing the physical vigor, say, of a housewives' bridge club with that of a student football team. Would the differences in vigor be caused by the innate differences between bridge players and ball players? We would be ignoring the full explanation if we didn't recognize the differences in the age and sex composition of the two groups. Standardization is simply a way of making this recognition.

What may we hope to learn by comparing the migrants with the groups they leave and the groups they join? If migrants' characteristics and experiences are indeed different from those of the rest of the population, then they merit further study as a special group with special problems and potentials. If not, then the labor problems of a developing society such as Chile should probably be considered without making artificial distinctions between migrants and nonmigrants.

Age and Sex Distribution

The most recent migrants, as Bogue and others infer, tend to be young adults. Table 6.1 gives relevant statistics on the age-sex distribution. Among the most recent migrants — those with fewer than ten years of residence in Greater Santiago — about two-fifths of those over fourteen years of age were between fifteen and twenty-four. Even more striking are the data on the age of migrants at the time of arrival, shown in Table 6.2. Almost one-third arrived during their late teen years. More than six out of ten were present in Santiago before their twenty-sixth birthday. The youth of the migrants is thus clearly demonstrated.

Ravenstein's generalization about the importance of women within the migration stream, made originally in the context of nineteenth-century England, was true for recent Chile as well.[2] Table 6.3 shows there were as few as 52 men for every 100 women within the recent migrants aged fifteen to twenty-four.[3] For adults (all those over fourteen), there were only 64 men for every 100 women.

The high ratio of women to men among the most recent migrants, not present among the older migrants, can be linked with the occupations and work histories of these recent migrants. Many young women come to Santiago, and the bulk of them enter domestic service. Domestic service is an unstable occupation, characterized by many small employers (that is, households which hire only one or two servants) and high turnover. Inevitably some of the migrant girls whose entire work experience in the city consists of domestic service become discouraged and return to their former homes. This accounts for the lowering of the sex ratio when the group of all migrants is considered: the return home of some of the female members of the recent migrant group pushes the ratio down.

The mobility of Chilean women indicates fundamental changes occurring within the society. The move to the cities for them means a transfer from places where employment opportunities are virtually nonexistent to places where women's jobs may be found. Women's participation rates in the rural sector of the economy in 1960 were 10.0%; in the urban sector, 27.2%.[4] Within Greater Santiago, female

[2] Ravenstein's "laws of migration" were treated in Chapter 2.

[3] Here, as before, a "recent" migrant is one with fewer than ten years of residence in Santiago.

[4] *Algunos resultados del XIII censo, op. cit.*, p. 14, using census definitions of urban and rural.

TABLE 6.1
AGE-SEX DISTRIBUTION: CHILE, 1960 AND GREATER SANTIAGO, 1963

Chile Outside Santiago

Ages	Numbers (in Thousands)			Percentage Distribution of Those over 14		
	Men	Women	Total	Men	Women	Total
0–14	1,115.1	1,090.7	2,205.8	—	—	—
15–24	490.1	473.5	963.6	30.6%	29.9%	30.3%
25–44	627.7	621.7	1,249.4	39.2	39.2	39.2
45–64	369.3	367.5	736.8	23.1	23.2	23.1
65+	112.1	123.2	235.3	7.0	7.8	7.4
Total	2,714.3	2,676.6	5,390.9	100.0%	100.0%	100.0%
Number over 14	1,599.2	1,585.9	3,185.1			

Greater Santiago — Natives

Ages	Numbers (in Thousands)			Percentage Distribution of Those over 14		
	Men	Women	Total	Men	Women	Total
0–14	342.4	334.4	676.8	—	—	—
15–24	133.5	142.5	276.0	40.7%	36.8%	38.6%
25–44	124.3	156.7	281.0	38.0	40.5	39.3
45–64	54.4	69.3	123.6	16.6	17.9	17.3
65+	13.3	15.6	28.9	4.1	4.0	4.0
No data	1.9	2.9	4.9	0.6	0.8	0.7
Total	669.8	721.4	1,391.2	100.0%	100.0%	100.0%
Number over 14	327.4	387.0	714.4			

TABLE 6.1 (Continued)

Greater Santiago — Migrants

Ages	Numbers (in Thousands)			Percentage Distribution of Those over 14		
	Men	Women	Total	Men	Women	Total
0 –14	33.1	35.4	68.5	—	—	—
15–24	50.9	85.8	136.8	16.8%	19.8%	18.5%
25–44	129.5	175.7	305.2	42.6	40.6	41.5
45–64	95.2	130.3	225.5	31.3	30.1	30.6
65+	27.6	39.4	67.0	9.1	9.1	9.1
No data	0.8	1.5	2.3	0.3	0.3	0.3
Total	337.2	468.1	805.3	100.0%	100.0%	100.0%
Number over 14	304.1	432.7	736.8			

Greater Santiago — Recent Migrants*

Ages	Numbers (in Thousands)			Percentage Distribution of Those over 14		
	Men	Women	Total	Men	Women	Total
0 –14	30.8	33.7	64.6	—	—	—
15–24	33.6	65.1	98.7	35.5%	40.1%	38.4%
25–44	45.4	69.3	114.7	48.0	42.7	44.7
45–64	13.5	21.3	34.7	14.2	13.1	13.5
65+	2.1	6.5	8.6	2.2	4.0	3.4
Total	125.4	195.8	321.3	100.0%	100.0%	100.0%
Number over 14	94.6	162.1	256.7			

Sources: Algunos resultados del XIII censo, op. cit., unpublished data of the Dirección de Estadística y Censos, and unpublished data from the June 1963 employment survey of the Institute of Economics of Santiago.

* "Recent migrants" are here defined as those migrants with ten or fewer years of residence in Greater Santiago.

TABLE 6.2

SANTIAGO: AGE AT ARRIVAL OF ECONOMICALLY ACTIVE RECENT MIGRANTS

Age Group	Per Cent of Migrants Arriving at That Age
0–5	1.3%
6–10	1.6
11–15	11.0
16–20	31.3
21–25	18.1
26–30	14.5
31–35	7.4
36–40	5.5
41–45	4.8
46–50	1.3
51–55	1.3
56–60	1.3
No data	0.6
Total	100.0%

Source: Survey of recent migrants described in Appendix B.

TABLE 6.3

CHILE: SEX RATIOS BY AGE GROUPS: NUMBER OF MEN PER 100 WOMEN

| Age Group | Outside Santiago | Greater Santiago | | |
		Natives	All Migrants	Recent Migrants
0–14	102	102	93	91
15–24	103	94	59	52
25–44	101	79	74	66
45–64	100	78	73	63
65 and over	91	85	70	32
All adults	101	93	72	64

Notes: "Recent" migrants are those with fewer than ten years of residence in Santiago. The data for outside Santiago refer to the year 1960, while those for Greater Santiago are for 1963.

Sources: For outside Santiago, Algunos resultados del XIII censo, op. cit., and unpublished data of the Dirección de Estadística y Censos. For Greater Santiago, unpublished data from the June 1963 employment survey of the Institute of Economics.

participation was even more energetic: 34.7%.[5] Thus the probability that any given Santiago woman would be a labor force participant was three and one-half times that for her rural cousin.[6]

[5] In June 1963, according to unpublished data of the employment survey of the Institute of Economics.

[6] These results should be considered with an understanding of the defi-

Education

Two seemingly conflicting hypotheses about the educational attainments of the migrants are plausible. The first maintains that the migrant, a fellow bright and alert to changing opportunities, mobile and flexible, has a "higher than average" level of education. The second hypothesis claims that the opportunities for education outside the biggest cities are so limited that potential migrants living in the countryside have little chance to avail themselves of an education which might help them greatly after they arrive in Santiago.

The educational superiority of Chile's urban areas (as defined by the census) is marked. In 1960, urban illiteracy, for instance, was 9.0% for those over 14, while the comparable rural figure, more than three times as high, was 31.0%.[7] For some provinces the percentage of urban students able to remain in school until their sixth grade graduation was more than six times as high as that for rural students.[8] And this comparison understates the differences between urban and rural education, since it deals only with the percentage of those matriculated in the first grade. In rural areas, relatively fewer children even start school, thus making their number smaller from the very beginning.

Both of the proposed hypotheses about migrants' education have a grain of truth in them. Table 6.4 shows that the migrants to Santiago are distinctly better educated than the people living outside

nitional exclusion of farm wives from the labor force. Suppose farm wives were considered active rather than inactive, by virtue of their caring for small vegetable gardens, tending livestock, engaging in spinning, etc. Although the number of farm wives (and daughters over fourteen) does not appear directly in the census, a rough calculation shows that the female participation rate in the rural sector could be 87.9% rather than the 10.0% which the census shows. This calculation first separates farm and nonfarm population within the rural sector by using the ratio of male agricultural labor force members to rural male actives in 1960 (0.881). Multiplying this ratio by the number of total rural women over fourteen approximates the number of active and inactive farm wives and daughters. Then this number of farm wives and daughters is assumed to have the same participation rate as rural men (92.4%). Since agriculture forms the bulk of the rural sector, the rural female participation rate emerges as the 87.9% stated above. Using one other assumption, that each agricultural wife and daughter (over fourteen) is equivalent to 0.6 males, the rural female participation rate is still as high as 55.3%, well above the Santiago rate of 34.7% noted in the text. This sensitivity of the female participation rate to changes in census definitions should be borne in mind.

[7] *Algunos resultados del XIII censo de población y II de vivienda* (Santiago: Dirección de Estadística y Censos, 1963), p. 11.

[8] Eduardo Hamuy et al., *El problema educacional del pueblo chileno* (Santiago, Editorial Universitaria, 1960), pp. 195–200.

Santiago. Whereas more than one-fifth of the non-Santiago residents were totally without formal instruction, only one-twelfth of Santiago's migrants were similarly handicapped. The migrants were more than five times as likely to have university training than those they left behind.

On the other hand, Table 6.4 also indicates the degree by which migrants lagged educationally behind the Santiago natives. Only

TABLE 6.4

CHILE: EDUCATIONAL ATTAINMENTS OF THE POPULATION MORE THAN 14 YEARS OLD, IN THOUSANDS

Highest Level of Education Reached	Outside Santiago 1960	Greater Santiago 1958	
		Natives	Migrants
No education	683.2	20.1	52.7
Primary education	1,818.5	279.8	317.0
Technical and special education	133.6	36.3	27.6
Secondary education	516.2	207.3	166.5
University education	33.6	26.0	34.8
Total	3,185.1	569.6	598.6

Percentage Distribution	Outside Santiago 1960	Greater Santiago 1958	
		Natives	Migrants
No education	21.4%	3.5%	8.8%
Primary education	57.1	49.1	53.0
Technical and special education	4.2	6.4	4.6
Secondary education	16.2	36.4	27.8
University education	1.1	4.6	5.8
Total	100.0%	100.0%	100.0%

Cumulative Percentage Distribution	Outside Santiago 1960	Greater Santiago 1958	
		Natives	Migrants
More than secondary education	1.1%	4.6%	5.8%
With at least secondary or technical education	21.5	47.4	38.2
With at least primary education	78.6	96.5	91.2

Sources: *Algunos resultados del XIII censo, op. cit.*, pp. 10, 11, 15; unpublished census data from the Dirección de Estadística y Censos; unpublished data from the labor force survey of the Institute of Economics for June 1958.

half as many of the natives were without education, and natives were more likely to have technical and secondary educations than were the migrants. The migrants surpassed them only in the relative number with university educations. This, of course, resulted from migrants coming to Santiago to get a university degree. In the process of obtaining specialized education, these most intelligent and potentially flexible migrants made their adjustments to urban life and remained in Santiago after graduation. In addition, in many specialized fields, the capital city was the site either of the only job opportunities open to the graduate or of the most attractive ones. Thus about 1% more of the migrants had college educations than did the Santiago natives.

The educational superiority of the natives might be explained by two separate factors. First, as we have seen in Table 6.3, the natives' ratio of women to men was lower in every age category. Since as a group women usually have less education than men, their lower proportion among the natives might lead to the natives' over-all educational advantage. Second, Table 6.1 showed that in the adult group with which we are concerned, the migrants tended to be older than the natives.[9] Owing to education's gains over time in most countries, the natives, relatively younger as a group than the migrants, would have had a better chance for education than the migrants.

How much of the natives' educational superiority can actually be traced to differences in the age and sex composition between them and the migrants, as these *a priori* objections have suggested? Table 6.5 gives us some idea. This table focuses on part of one group, the economically active males in Greater Santiago, and classifies them according to place of birth (i.e., native or migrant), age, and education. As the table shows, the most dramatic differences between native and migrant now disappear. For every class of education, the gap between the natives and migrants has been narrowed simply by considering only the economically active men of *all* ages. Furthermore, within *each* age group the natives and migrants became even more alike. In the youngest group being considered (aged fifteen to twenty-four), for example, an almost exactly equal percentage of the native and migrant men had primary and secondary

---

[9] Although migrants are young when they arrive, the long average length of residence shown in Chapter 4 and the low number arriving in any given year mean that the adult migrants are *older* as a group than the natives, not younger.

education. As in the over-all comparison, however, the natives retained their advantage in technical schooling and the migrants theirs in university education.

TABLE 6.5

GREATER SANTIAGO: EDUCATIONAL ATTAINMENTS OF ECONOMICALLY ACTIVE MALES OVER 14 YEARS OLD, 1958

Highest Educational Level Reached	Place of Birth	Age			
		15–24	25–44	45–64	Total*
Without education	Native	2.0%	2.3%	5.3%	2.7%
	Migrant	2.6	4.0	8.8	5.5
Primary education	Native	58.4	51.5	45.7	52.5
	Migrant	58.6	53.5	44.1	51.6
Technical and special education	Native	8.7	4.9	8.2	6.5
	Migrant	4.6	6.5	6.7	6.2
Secondary education	Native	29.5	34.2	32.2	32.4
	Migrant	29.6	28.1	31.8	29.0
University education	Native	1.4	7.1	8.7	5.8
	Migrant	4.6	8.0	8.6	7.7
Total	Native	100.0%	100.0%	100.0%	100.0%
	Migrant	100.0%	100.0%	100.0%	100.0%

* Total includes those people over 65.

Source: Unpublished data from the labor force survey of the Institute of Economics for June 1958.

The standardization by age and sex thus shows that the average young male migrant was not likely to be educationally handicapped in his job search. The natives who were his competitors for available positions did not have a statistically significant edge over him in educational attainments.

Participation Rates

As with education, the migrants' rates of participation in the labor force might be hypothesized to be either higher or lower than the natives' rates.[10] Higher, if it is thought that migrants as a whole are somehow more energetic and spirited than the natives; lower, if the

[10] For the purposes of this study,

$$\text{Participation rate} \equiv \frac{\text{labor force}}{\text{population over 14}}$$

$$\text{Age-specific participation rate} \equiv \frac{\text{labor force in an age group}}{\text{population in that age group}}$$

migrants are thought to be lazier or more easily discouraged by the complexities of city life. Table 6.6 allows us to decide between these views.

Taken as an aggregate, the migrants' participation rate was higher, by a statistically significant margin,[11] than that of the natives. In each of the disaggregated age groups the participation rate was also higher for the migrants than for the natives, although the margins in the older groups were not significant. The migrants' rate approached the natives' as older groups were considered. The explanation is straightforward. The migrants and natives are likely to be most dissimilar at the time the migrants arrive in Santiago, i.e., in the youngest age groups. As the migrants age and as their exposure to life in the capital increases, their behavior comes more and more to resemble that of the natives. Their participation rate reflects the growing similarity between the two groups.

This interpretation is strengthened by the pattern of age-specific participation rates of the people living outside Santiago. The migrants and those they left behind had almost equal rates in the age group from fifteen to nineteen, the age at which most of the migrants were newly arrived in the big city. It is in precisely this age group that the migrants and people outside Santiago should most resemble each other, and it is intellectually satisfying that they in fact did so. In the ages from twenty to forty-four, a greater female participation in Santiago drove the migrants' rate above that of those outside Santiago. Finally, in the oldest groups, participation of Santiago residents, migrants, and natives alike, fell below that of the non-Santiago population. People did not remain in the work force as long in Santiago as outside, owing to "competitive employment practices, retirement funds, and urban and industrial conditions which impede the economic activity" of older people in the capital.[12]

Further illumination about the nature of participation is provided by data on the age-sex specific participation rates of migrants and natives. Table 6.7 shows that participation rates for the men were nearly equal in all ages, and over-all migrant participation did not exceed that of the natives by a statistically significant amount. For

[11] The probability is 95% that the error in the total participation rates for the natives and migrants is no more than 2.7% of the measured rates.

[12] United Nations, Economic Commission for Latin America, "The Demographic Situation in Latin America," *Economic Bulletin for Latin America*, Vol. 6, No. 2 (October 1961), 43.

TABLE 6.6
TOTAL POPULATION (OVER 14 YEARS OLD), ECONOMICALLY ACTIVE POPULATION, AND PARTICIPATION RATES

Ages		Chile, 1960		Ages	Greater Santiago, 1963	
		Santiago	Outside Santiago		Natives	Migrants
15–19	pop'n.	189.6	539.5	15–19	151.7	61.5
	ec. act.	74.9	241.3		45.3	27.6
20–29	pop'n.	325.8	797.7	20–34	287.8	235.6
	ec. act.	203.6	482.5		177.7	155.3
30–44	pop'n.	381.4	875.8	35–44	117.5	144.9
	ec. act.	231.7	512.6		74.0	93.9
45–64	pop'n.	280.3	736.8	45–64	123.6	225.5
	ec. act.	139.3	384.9		62.5	115.4
65+	pop'n.	78.6	235.3	65+	28.9	67.0
	ec. act.	15.7	69.5		6.3	14.8
Total	pop'n.	1,255.7	3,185.1	Total	709.5	734.5
	ec. act.	655.2	1,690.8		365.7	406.9
		Participation Rates			*Participation Rates*	
15–19		39.5%	44.7%	15–19	29.8%	44.9%
20–29		62.5	60.5	20–34	61.7	65.9
30–44		60.8	58.5	35–44	63.0	64.8
45–64		49.7	52.2	45–64	50.5	51.2
65+		20.0	29.5	65+	21.9	22.0
Total		53.0%	53.1%	Total	51.5%	55.4%

Sources: *Algunos resultados del XIII censo, op. cit.,* p. 14; unpublished census data from the Dirección de Estadística y Censos; unpublished data from the June 1963 labor force survey of the Institute of Economics.
Note: Numbers in the population and the labor force are in thousands.

the women, on the other hand, a contrasting situation was provided, in which participation of the migrants was higher in total and in each of the age groups, the differences in most age groups being significant.

TABLE 6.7
GREATER SANTIAGO: LABOR FORCE PARTICIPATION RATES, 1963

Age Group	Men		Women	
	Natives	*Migrants*	*Natives*	*Migrants*
15–19	41.1%	43.8%	19.4%	45.7%
20–24	78.8	81.5	40.7	59.4
25–34	99.8	94.9	36.6	47.0
35–44	96.4	93.4	34.2	38.6
45–64	80.9	78.9	26.7	30.9
65+	36.6	40.0	9.4	9.5
All adults	76.4%	79.5%	30.5%	38.4%

Source: Unpublished data from the labor force survey of the Institute of Economics for June 1963.

The explanation for higher participation among the migrant women is clear. Although about two-thirds of them came accompanying the family's breadwinner or to study at a Santiago school, the remaining third had some economic interest in migrating to Santiago.[13] And indeed their participation rate was something more than one-third (38.4% in 1963). Again the greatest differences between migrants and natives lay in the youngest age groups, before the complete adjustment to Santiago life or the assimilation of urban cultural values had been made.

Localizing the differences in migrants' and natives' participation rates thus helps us to understand further the nature of the migratory process. The men, taken by age groups, did not exhibit different economic behavior according to whether they were born within or outside of Santiago. The migrant women, on the other hand, were more likely to be active within the Santiago labor force. Many of them came to Santiago precisely because the city offered them employment opportunities that were not available or were less attractive in their place of origin. Inactive before they came, they now entered into economic activity. In contrast, the men presum-

[13] Institute of Economics, *La población del Gran Santiago* (Santiago, 1959), p. 110. Although this study's reasons for migration were criticized in an earlier chapter (Chapter 2), the usefulness of its results are illustrated by this example.

ably would have been active in some kind of work whether they
were in Santiago or outside it.

Unemployment

The cornerstone of much of the impressionistic writing on internal
migration has been the high degree of unemployment of the migrants. According to these expositions, underemployment on the
farms is replaced, after rural-urban migration, by massive unemployment in the cities. The truly pitiable living conditions of a few
unemployed migrant families are usually cited as a reason to con-
demn the flood of humanity to the largest cities.

One of the central purposes of this study, then, is to compare
unemployment in the migrant and native groups and to try to
explain any differences found.[14] Possibly the most surprising finding,
shown in Table 6.8, is that *migrants had a lower, not a higher, rate*

TABLE 6.8

CHILE: UNEMPLOYMENT AS A PERCENTAGE OF THE LABOR FORCE

| Group | Outside Santiago 1960 | Group | Greater Santiago 1963 | |
			Natives	Migrants
Men	7.1%	Men	7.2%	4.6%
Women	4.6	Women	4.9	3.1

| Ages | Outside Santiago 1960 | Ages | Greater Santiago 1963 | |
			Natives	Migrants
15–19	15.5	15–19	14.0	8.8
20–29	6.6	20–34	6.4	4.8
30–44	4.7	35–44	3.5	3.6
45–64	4.2	45–64	4.9	2.4
65+	4.9	65+	2.6	2.2
Total	6.7%	Total	6.4%	4.0%

Sources: Tables 5.1 and 5.3 and unpublished data from the employment
survey of the Institute of Economics for June 1963.

of unemployment than the Santiago natives. Whereas the natives
had rates comparable with those of non-Santiago residents, the
migrants of both sexes and in almost all age groups had lower rates
than either the Santiago natives or the people living outside San-

[14] Differences in unemployment experience between Santiago and the rest
of Chile were explored in the previous chapter.

tiago. The migrants were hardly a group on the fringes of society and the economy. Not only were they participating in the labor force to a somewhat greater extent than were the natives, as shown in the last section, but in addition their job searches were more likely to be rewarded with jobs.

The success of the migrants in coping with the danger of (measured) unemployment is also shown by a comparison of their unemployment rates with those of the population of Chile living outside Santiago. The patterns were similar to the comparison between Santiago natives and the migrants: for both men and women and in every age group, the unemployment of the migrants fell below that of the people they left behind.[15]

Clearly, within the Chilean context of interurban migration and economic stagnation, the views about migrants and unemployment stated in the first paragraph of this section must be revised. Whatever problems the migrants and the society around them faced, an extraordinarily high rate of measured unemployment was not one of them.

Occupational Distribution of the Labor Force

The occupational distribution of the labor force helps explain some of the differences found in unemployment rates between migrants and natives. In general, if the distributions were similar for the two groups, the unemployment rate differences would then gain real interest. If, on the other hand, the occupational distributions of the natives and migrants differed significantly, and if global unemployment were considered as a weighted average of sectoral unemployment, then it follows that the group with a relatively larger number of workers in sectors with low unemployment rates would have a lower over-all rate of unemployment.

The empirical evidence helps us decide between these two alter-

15 These comparisons are qualified somewhat by the decline in measured unemployment in Greater Santiago between 1960 when the census was taken and 1963 when the labor survey used for the comparison was made. Results on the same order of magnitude, however, were obtained when data for the 1957 and 1958 labor force surveys were used. These are shown in the following table:

Greater Santiago: Unemployment Rates

Date	Natives	Migrants
June 1957	8%	5%
June 1958	10.8%	8.3%

natives. Table 6.9 presents the occupational distribution of the labor force, disaggregated by sex and place of birth (i.e., natives and migrants). To survey the issue further, the results of the labor force surveys taken on two different dates are shown in the table.

TABLE 6.9

GREATER SANTIAGO: OCCUPATIONAL DISTRIBUTION OF THE LABOR FORCE

| | Men | | | |
| | June 1958 | | June 1963 | |
Occupation	Natives	Migrants	Natives	Migrants
Professionals and technicians	6.1%	5.4%	8.0%	10.3%
Owners and managers	5.5	7.7	9.3	14.5
Office workers	10.8	8.4	11.4	11.6
Salesmen	10.5	10.3	12.1	9.7
Farmers and miners	1.4	2.5	1.3	2.1
Drivers and deliverymen	6.4	7.6	7.5	5.0
Artisans and operatives	41.9	40.1	35.1	29.5
Unskilled manual workers	5.8	4.9	4.6	4.8
Personal service workers	8.8	10.9	7.9	11.3
Unclassified	1.6	1.6	1.6	0.9
Seeking work for the first time	1.2	0.5	1.2	0.3
Total	100.0%	100.0%	100.0%	100.0%

| | Women | | | |
| | June 1958 | | June 1963 | |
Occupation	Natives	Migrants	Natives	Migrants
Professionals and technicians	6.7%	5.0%	10.7%	8.8%
Owners and managers	1.9	1.5	5.7	3.9
Office workers	12.7	8.1	15.4	9.2
Sales personnel	12.0	8.2	11.2	7.6
Artisans and operatives	33.8	22.3	22.9	15.1
Personal service workers	30.1	51.7	30.5	54.0
Otherwise classified	0.8	1.1	1.4	0.7
Seeking work for the first time	2.1	2.1	2.2	0.7
Total	100.0%	100.0%	100.0%	100.0%

Sources: Unpublished data from the employment surveys of the Institute of Economics.

This much is clear: more native men worked as artisans and operatives, while more migrants found employment (or employed themselves) as owners and managers and as personal service workers. These differences, present in 1958, were even more pronounced in 1963.[16] The ease of entry into the services and the low measured rate of unemployment in that branch of activity undoubtedly had their effect on lowering the over-all rate of unemployment of migrants. Owners, especially of small family enterprises, are very seldom unemployed in the measured sense of actively seeking work. This would also have its effect on the migrants' over-all unemployment. The natives' higher rate of unemployment was consistent with their bulge in the artisans-and-operatives category, since most of these people would work in manufacturing and construction where unemployment rates were typically higher (as shown in Chapter 5).

Migrant and native women exhibited occupational patterns similar to those of the men. More natives found work in offices and as operatives. Migrants dominated personal service employment, the bulk of which was domestic service. Thus, as with the men, there were more natives in branches with high unemployment rates and more migrants in branches with low rates. The effects on the over-all rate follow arithmetically: the natives suffered a higher global rate of unemployment; the migrants, a lower one.

It is easy, however, to overemphasize the differences between the migrant and native groups in the occupational distribution. Just as notable as these differences, in my opinion, were their similarities. These similarities reflected the long length of residence of the majority of the migrants. Not many of the migrants were "new" migrants and Chilean urban life with its somewhat underdeveloped industrial pattern did not force all these migrants or even a statistically significant portion of them into occupations different from those of the natives.

Conclusions

How different were the migrants from the natives? The evidence cited in this chapter allows the conclusion that they were really very similar when considered as whole groups. Within these groups, however, significant differences emerged.

[16] On the other hand, some differences present in 1958 had become weaker or reversed themselves by 1963. In 1958, more native men than migrant men were professionals; in 1963, the reverse was true. The same occurred with office workers. The opposite pattern appeared among drivers and unskilled manual workers: the migrants' 1958 predominance had been reversed by 1963. The big difference between these reversals and the distributional patterns outlined in Table 6.9 is that none of the differences between migrants and natives noted in this footnote are statistically significant, owing to the size of the sample. Of course, that fact in itself has some interest: what is being said is that for statistical purposes the *same* proportion of migrants and natives were, for example, professionals, or office workers, or manual workers in 1963.

Perhaps the most striking difference affecting the development process is the mobility of women. Migrant women displayed a surprising degree of participation in the labor force. Much of their activity might be considered wasted for strict development purposes, since nonprofessional personal services claimed a majority of them. Nevertheless, their interest and ability to leave their former homes and come to Santiago to work means that real industrialization in Santiago would have this large group of women potentially available to it. Impressionistic evidence further strongly suggests that industrial wages higher than maids' wages and the freedom from domineering household masters would prove powerful attractions, serving to deflect this stream of migrant women away from domestic service and into the factories.

The migrant men, on the other hand, displayed few differences from their Santiago-born brothers. A few more, to be sure, were in the personal services or were self-employed "owners" with a correspondingly lower productivity, but these differences were not large enough to be impressive. It therefore seems labored, at least within the Chilean context, to treat the migrant men as a group deserving of special attention because of their supposed disadvantages when compared with natives.

7

Social and Occupational Experience of the Migrants

Migration will be more efficient as an allocator of economic resources if the migrant is easily accepted into the urban culture and if he in turn accepts it. This assumption is basic to the chapter that follows. Of course, the concept at issue here is very closely related to labor commitment.

> A committed worker is one who stays on the job, and who has severed his major connections with the land. He is a permanent member of the industrial working force, receiving wages and being dependent for making a living on enterprise managements which offer him work and direct his activities at the work place.[1]

In a detailed description, commitment means

> *both* the short-run objective performance of modern kinds of economic activity *and* the long-run and deep-seated acceptance of the attitudes and beliefs appropriate to a modernized economy.[2]

Clearly labor commitment as described in these statements is a concomitant of the process of industrial development. Within certain wide limits, the more intensely workers are committed to the processes of industrialization and urbanization, the faster these processes will occur. But because of the problems of adjustment to

[1] Clark Kerr, *et al.*, *Industrialism and Industrial Man* (Cambridge, Mass.: Harvard University Press, 1960), p. 170.
[2] Wilbert E. Moore and Arnold S. Feldman (eds.), *Labor Commitment and Social Change in Developing Areas* (New York: Social Science Research Council, 1960), v. Emphasis in original.

urban life, the lack of facilities for effective industrial training, and the proliferation of " 'primitive' tertiary industries" and " 'nonmarket' urban services,"

> the emphasis here on mobility as an essential feature of labor market development is . . . something more than the requirement for "bodies." Movement [by the migrants] into the market sector is itself problematical and still leaves uncertain the further performance of appropriate kind and quality that characterizes a developed labor market.[3]

Movement, reflected in urbanization, is thus not enough to guarantee development. Problems of postmovement commitment remain. This chapter proposes to explore the degree of commitment exhibited by Santiago migrants and to relate it to its expected results on economic development.

Arrival

What problems might the migrant face before getting to the capital? How will he fare when he arrives? The answers to these questions shed light on the nature of migration and on its economic effects. In an attempt to gain some insight into these problems, we surveyed 310 economically active migrants who had arrived in Santiago within the last ten years. The technical details about the selection of the sample, the pretest, the questionnaire, etc., appear in Appendix B. We questioned these migrants about their employment and personal experiences before and after arrival in Santiago. Their responses revealed details about their lives which differed considerably from those of migrants in some other low-income countries.

Adjustment to life in the big city will presumably be easier the more the migrant knows about it in advance. Previous visits to the capital would provide at least a glimpse of the type of life and problems to be encountered by a Santiago resident. More than half of the recent migrants surveyed had been in Santiago at least once before moving there to stay. Some of them tried to shrug off this exposure to Santiago life, saying "I was only here on my vacation" or "I just looked around and went home." Nevertheless it seems clear that internal migrants in some developing countries do not have a level of income high enough (nor the sort of employment situation)

---

[3] *Ibid.*, pp. 49–50.

to allow them to take vacations or to make reconnaissance trips to the city before moving there definitely. In addition, it is easy to imagine some people coming to Santiago "on vacation" and being repelled by the type of life they observed there. The population redistribution within the country is therefore more efficient if these people, who without preliminary knowledge might have moved, use their brief exposure to Santiago to discourage themselves from living there. The alternative and probably less efficient pattern of movement would include waves of migration and backward migration by the same people.

Another indication of the amount of information about city life available to the migrants comes from the number who have friends and relatives living in the city prior to their own arrival there. A surprising 83.9% of the recent migrants had friends or relatives already living in Santiago who could potentially provide them with information about a cross section of local job opportunities and other urban economic conditions.

In addition, the costs of migration for the migrant are lowered when these Santiago residents provide the migrants with free lodging and food. It has been remarked that the *allegado*[4] is a Chilean institution. Visits of indefinite length by these relatives are not unusual.

Finally, in a country with a modern railway network extending both north and south through the most heavily populated zones, it is not surprising that a large fraction (62.3%) of the migrants came to Santiago by train. In addition, another 21.3% came either by bus or truck.[5] Costs to the migrants for travel by any of these three means of transport are very low. Government subsidies of railway passenger fares, whether as a conscious policy measure or not, create a ceiling above which truck or bus fares may not go without speedy effects on passenger volume.[6] This downward pressure by the government on passenger fares, insofar as it lowered the cost of migration and insofar as migration was sensitive to direct money costs, reinforced the stimuli to Santiago migration.

[4] Here, the relative or friend from out of town living with the family.

[5] I suspect that the number coming by truck may be understated. Those who did admit that they came in a truck seemed embarrassed to say so, since there is not much *dignidad* attached to a long journey in the back of a truck.

[6] Robert T. Brown and Carlos Hurtado R.-T. have commented on the peculiar economics of Chilean transportation and have suggested some alternative arrangements in their *Una política de transportes para Chile* (Santiago: Institute of Economics, 1963).

Employment after Arrival

Migration's effectiveness as a method of labor allocation depends in part on the length of time necessary for the migrant to find his first steady job and on the number of jobs he holds during his initial period in the city. The underlying assumption, of course, is that the longer the period of unemployment, the higher the cost to the migrant of his move.

Of the economically active recent migrants surveyed, about four-fifths were active members of the labor force immediately upon arrival. The others were students, housewives, or other inactives who only later entered the labor force. Of the four-fifths who sought work immediately upon arrival in Santiago, 40.6% found employment without delay. "Without delay" means that the migrants were employed either on the day they arrived or on the following day.[7] The following table shows details of the delays in encountering work:

Lag Between Arrival in Santiago and Employment in First Permanent Job	Percentage of Respondents
No delay	40.6%
1 week or less	6.7
2 weeks	5.5
3 to 4 weeks	9.8
Less than one month	62.7%
2 to 3 months	10.2%
4 to 6 months	7.9
Between one month and six months	18.1%
7 months to 1 year	8.7%
More than 1 year to less than 2 years	3.1
More than 2 years	2.0
More than 6 months	13.8%
No response	5.5%
Total	100.0%

The table shows that, although most — about five-eighths — of the migrants found steady jobs with delays as short as one month or less, there was also a hard core of workers — almost 14% — who actively sought permanent employment for six months or longer without finding it. In addition to their lack of success in their search

[7] When a surveyed migrant told us that he had found work *al tiro* (right away), we always questioned him closely, to get an estimate in number of days or weeks.

for a permanent job, fewer than half of these long-term unemployed people had even had casual jobs (*pololos, pololitos,* or *trabajitos*) during their initial period in Santiago. Thus there was a considerable spread among the migrants in the period of time spent unemployed.

A high degree of labor turnover among the migrants would also indicate some degree of maladjustment to the urban employment environment. If migrants changed jobs frequently, especially during their initial period in Santiago, the costs of migration would be higher than if steady employment were obtained. Furthermore the employers' costs in administration and training would exceed those engendered by a more stable employment situation. Admittedly, some degree of labor turnover is necessary to insure the fluidity which characterizes any perfect market, but beyond some point, excessive job shifts by new workers would lessen the over-all effectiveness of the migration process.

As might by now be expected, labor turnover among recent migrants to Santiago was not alarmingly high. Almost three-quarters held only one job during their first year in the capital. Only about 4%, by contrast, held three or more different jobs during their first year. We should interpret these results, however, with the knowledge that fully 11% of the migrants surveyed were unemployed during the whole of their first year in Santiago.

A great deal of diversity is thus shown in the migrants' ability to find work soon after arrival and in their capability to hold a steady job. To name a rough but convenient fraction, about three-quarters of the recent active migrants were shown by this investigation to have little initial difficulty in getting or keeping a job.[8] The other quarter, on the other hand, had a fairly prolonged period of unemployment after arrival or found themselves shunted between one employer and another, losing the money and other benefits that come with longer periods of uninterrupted employment.

Occupational Histories

In its survey of migrants who had arrived in Santiago within the last twenty years, the Latin American Demographic Center (CELADE) asked active migrants what jobs they had held before coming to Santiago, immediately after arrival, and now (i.e., at the

[8] See Appendix B for a complete tabulation of the results.

time of the survey, April 1962). Their responses indicated the degree of engagement of the migrants in the more advanced sectors of the economy after arrival. Table 7.1 details CELADE's findings.

As might be expected, the results show considerable shifts among occupations and from economic inactivity to employment. Among the currently employed men, nearly a quarter (22.5%) were economically inactive, seeking work for the first time, or unpaid family workers immediately before coming to Santiago. Immediately afterward, only 2.9% were similarly unoccupied. The white-collar work force almost doubled from less than one-fifth (17.9%) to more than one-third (35.3%). Not surprisingly the number of farmers (*agricultores*) shrank to one-tenth of its former size.[9]

The largest changes among the men's classifications were in the ranks of the blue-collar workers. Before coming to Santiago, 21.9% worked as blue-collar workers with various degrees of skill. This group included all the men from unskilled *cargadores* to highly skilled electricians and mechanics. From 21.9%, blue-collar workers increased to 40.2% after arrival in Santiago and to 47.9% at the time of the survey. It is clear that they made up the bulk of the migrant work force.

Finally, the group of men working in the various services also increased, but without such dramatic rapidity or magnitude.

The occupational histories of the women migrants confirmed once again one widely held impression: almost half of them (49.0%) were working in domestic service. Another 7.8% were employed in the other personal services as hairdressers, manicurists, and the like. Before coming to Santiago, on the other hand, only about one-fourth of them (24.4%) had been in domestic and personal service.

The expansion of white-collar employment among the women, as professional people, managers, saleswomen, and office workers, was of the same relative magnitude as the growth in the services, even though it did not involve such large numbers. Only 10.0% of the women practiced white-collar trades before coming to Santiago. Afterward the proportion grew to 27.1%.

As noted in earlier chapters, many of the women working in San-

---

[9] A legitimate question might be: How can there be farmers *inside* a modern urban metropolis of 2,000,000 people? The answer is that in addition to small orchard plots falling within the defined area of Greater Santiago, servants who work as gardeners are sometimes classed in these occupational surveys as *agricultores*, the same class into which rural cultivators of larger scale units would also be placed.

TABLE 7.1
GREATER SANTIAGO: MIGRANTS' OCCUPATIONAL HISTORIES[*]

Occupation	Before Coming to Santiago	After Arrival	Now (1962)
	Men		
Economically inactive, seeking work for the first time, and non-paid family workers	22.5%	2.9%	0.0%
Professionals, managers, salesmen, office workers	17.9	27.8	35.3
Farmers	18.1	2.7	2.0
Blue-collar workers, skilled and semi-skilled	19.9	32.4	41.2
Blue-collar workers, unskilled	2.0	7.8	6.7
Domestic service employees	1.6	2.5	2.2
Other personal service workers	5.1	11.0	12.3
Others	13.0	12.8	0.4
Total	100.0%	100.0%	100.0%
	Women		
Economically inactive, seeking work for the first time, and non-paid family workers	52.9%	2.7%	0.2%
Professionals, managers, salesmen, office workers	10.0	22.6	27.1
Farmers	1.2	0.2	0.7
Blue-collar workers, skilled and semi-skilled	4.8	9.5	14.4
Blue-collar workers, unskilled	0.0	0.5	0.5
Domestic service employees	22.0	53.4	49.0
Other personal service	2.4	4.6	7.8
Other	6.6	6.3	0.2
Total	100.0%	100.0%	100.0%
	Total		
Economically inactive, seeking work for the first time, and non-paid family workers	35.4%	2.8%	0.0%
Professionals, managers, salesmen, office workers	14.5	25.6	31.7
Farmers	10.9	1.7	1.5
Blue-collar workers, skilled and semi-skilled	13.5	22.7	29.8
Blue-collar workers, unskilled	1.1	4.7	4.0
Domestic service employees	10.3	24.2	22.1
Other personal service workers	3.9	8.3	10.6
Other	10.3	10.0	0.2
Total	100.0%	100.0%	100.0%

[*] Considered in this table are the migrants who came to Santiago during the period 1942–1962 and who are currently (1962) economically active.

Source: unpublished data of the Centro Latinoamericano de Demografía (CELADE).

tiago were not economically active in the towns they came from. More than half the women now at work (in 1962) were not working or were unpaid family workers or were definitionally excluded from the labor force as farm wives before coming to Santiago.

Combining the figures for both sexes, we see that of those at work in Santiago now, more than one-third (35.4%) were not working for pay in the place from which they came. For one reason or another, they traded inactivity in their home towns for economic activity in Santiago. It would be interesting to know how many migrant labor force members would have remained outside the labor force if they had not come to Santiago. As seen in Chapter 6, most migrants came to Santiago at about the age at which economic activity is usually begun, viz., during the late teen years. By far the majority of these people would have been active in their towns if they had somehow been denied the chance to come to Santiago. On the other hand, there must be some fraction, especially among the women, who would have remained outside the labor force if they had stayed at home. The Santiago labor market, with its facilities for the more ready placement of females, undoubtedly played its part in increasing participation rates and in the attractiveness of Santiago as a place to live.

Adjustment Problems

Within the wider range of social adjustment problems, the assumption made at the beginning of this chapter holds with undiminished strength. That is, the fewer the adjustment problems encountered by the Santiago migrant, the fewer will be the distractions diverting his attention and energies into social unrest.

The urban adjustment problems which migrants in other countries have faced range over a long and depressing list. Housing, family problems, crime, and delinquency are the most frequently mentioned in the literature.[10] Recalling what we have already dis-

[10] An interesting sample of the sorts of urban adjustment problems encountered can be found in the following works, listed with their country of reference:

MEXICO: Oscar Lewis, *Five Families — Mexican Case Studies in the Culture of Poverty* (New York: Science Editions, 1962)

CHILE: Carlos Munizaga A., *Estructuras transicionales en la migración de los araucanos de hoy a la ciudad de Santiago de Chile* (Santiago: University of Chile, 1961)

PERU: José Matos Mar, "Migration and Urbanization — The 'Barriadas' of

covered about the nature of the Santiago migrants, we might guess that the amount of social dislocation which they suffer would be less than that undergone by migrants in a country where *rural-urban* migration was a more common pattern than *interurban* migration. The present section will try to substantiate this view.

One of the most pressing urban problems which troubles Santiago is a shortage of adequate housing. As in Rio de Janeiro, Lima, and other Latin American cities, shantytowns have sprung up as the people attempt to alleviate the pressure on available housing. The colorful slang terms for these shantytowns — in Chile they are called *callampas* (mushrooms) — do not mask the misery which pervades them. It is commonly asserted that the newly arrived migrants form the majority of the residents within these *callampas*. The marginal nature of the migrants and their way of life is then "deduced" from this major premise.

A study by the U.N.'s Economic Commission for Latin America (ECLA) of the Santiago *callampas* has altered this stereotyped view of the migrants as a majority of a large subsistence sector within the urban society.[11] Extracted from a lengthy work by Guillermo Rosenblüth, the study reported on a survey of living conditions within the Santiago shantytowns.

Of primary interest was the survey's finding that the relative number of migrants living within the *callampas* approximated their proportion in the population of Greater Santiago as a whole. In Chapter 4 it was noted that migrants form more than one-third of Santiago's population, and after suitable corrections for the age distribution, it appears that a similar fraction of the *callampa* population was born outside Santiago. Although there was some evidence

Lima: An Example of Integration into Urban Life" in *Urbanization in Latin America* (Paris: UNESCO, 1961), pp. 170–190.

INDIA: Charles A. Myers, *Labor Problems in the Industrialization of India* (Cambridge, Mass.: Harvard University Press, 1958); and P. N. Prabhu, "Bombay: A Study of the Social Effects of Urbanization on Industrial Workers Migrating from the Rural Areas to the City of Bombay," in *The Social Implications of Industrialization and Urbanization: Five Studies of Urban Populations of Recent Rural Origin in Cities of Southern Asia* (Calcutta, UNESCO, 1956)

IRAQ: Doris G. Phillips, "Rural-to-Urban Migration in Iraq," *Economic Development and Cultural Change*, Vol. 7, No. 4 (July 1959), 405–421.

AFRICA: Walter Elkan, "Migrant Labor in Africa: An Economist's Approach," *American Economic Review*, Vol. 49, No. 2 (May 1959), 188–197.

[11] United Nations, Economic Commission for Latin America, "Urbanization in Latin America — Results of a Field Survey of Living Conditions in an Urban Sector," E/CN.12/662, 1963. Mimeographed.

suggesting that the proportion of rural migrants was higher in *callampas* than in the city as a whole, sampling problems made these results somewhat questionable.

In addition to being proportionately no more numerous than in the rest of the city, the migrants living in *callampas* had an impressive history of residence in Santiago. The following table shows dates at which the migrants living in the surveyed *callampas* came to Santiago.[12]

Date of Migration to Santiago	Percentage of Respondents
Before 1930	12%
1930–1939	13
1940–1949	25
1950–1959	29
Since 1960	6
Without data	15
Total	100%

Thus at least half the migrants had more than ten years of residence in Santiago, a figure tolerably close to the experience of all Santiago's migrants, as measured by the employment survey of the Institute of Economics and reported in Table 4.4.

The ECLA survey found, therefore, that migrants, especially those most recently arrived, were no more prevalent in the shantytowns than they were in the city of Santiago as a whole. The Commission concluded from these findings

> that the *callampas* represent a rejection by the city of elements already living in it, whether born there or not, and differing from the rest of the urban population more in degree of poverty than in origin.[13]

In response to the pressing problems of urban housing, the government of Chile during the administration of Jorge Alessandri Rodríguez (1958–1964) initiated a program of public housing. This program was supported by public revenues and offered modest dwellings of varying sizes to low income citizens. Ownership rather than mere tenancy was a goal of the program, and the houses (or apartments) carried long-term, low-interest mortgages. In an attempt to make the program eventually self-supporting, mortgage payments were readjustable (upward), the amount of the readjustment depending on indices of price or wage increases. Thus it was

[12] *Ibid.*, p. 16. The date of the survey was October 1962.
[13] *Ibid.*, p. 15.

hoped that inflation would not make repayments, ordinarily fixed in money terms rather than real terms, lower than the amount of new loans after an initial period.[14]

The people living in housing provided by the Housing Corporation (Corporación de la Vivienda, CORVI, the public housing authority) in many cases had moved to the new tracts from the *callampas*. Others had come from over-crowded central city housing (*conventillos*). Although CORVI housing was modest, every dwelling was at least provided with running water and with minimal kitchen and bathroom facilities.

Part of the housing program included a provision for social workers to ease the adjustment problems of the CORVI householders to their new homes. These social workers, for the most part young and middle-aged women, were a fertile source of information about the problems faced by people who move from the lowest urban stratum into the one second from the bottom.

Interviews with CORVI's social workers revealed, however, that the problems of the migrants within the new housing districts were no different than those of natives living there. The migrants received no special treatment; no different techniques had evolved among the social workers to deal with problems which seemed to arise with special frequency among migrants simply because there appeared to be no such problems.

[14] An interesting glimpse into the everyday problems faced by a developing economy is offered by an episode surrounding the readjustments of these mortgage payments. The Chilean Congress in 1963 could not agree on the amount of the readjustment. Although year-end wage increases were effective during the first quarter of 1963, debate dragged on until May about the size of the necessary or desirable readjustment. In general, party lines shaped the debate: the right lauded "financial responsibility" and favored a readjustment in the full amount of the price increases of the previous year. The left, on the other hand, feigned money illusion. As a result, the left opposed such a large readjustment, portraying the workers who held mortgages as being burdened by monetary obligations of ever increasing size. The delay in the passage of the 1963 readjustment meant that workers had the opportunity to adjust their family budgets to their new 1963 wages without an increase in necessary mortgage payments during the first half of 1963. When the readjustment was finally passed, the complaints against it were therefore numerous — so numerous in fact that payment of the new rates was first postponed until October 1 and finally until January 1 of the following year. Newspaper accounts of this debate, especially as carried in the conservative *Mercurio* and left wing tabloid *Clarín*, are not only colorful but informative about the problems of the interaction between political exigencies and economic progress. On a more general level, these issues are explored in a provocative work by Albert Hirschman, *Journeys Toward Progress — Studies of Economic Policy-Making in Latin America* (New York: Twentieth Century Fund, 1963).

The CORVI housing developments (*poblaciones*) had files listing family and occupational characteristics of the residents.[15] One district had circulated lists of its residents' job qualifications to members of the Sociedad de Fomento Fabril (the Chilean equivalent of the National Association of Manufacturers). This process resulted in some success in obtaining jobs for the residents. The social workers said that they could ascertain no discrimination between migrants and natives when people were hired.

Conclusions

Two main conclusions emerge from this chapter. The first concerns the costs of migration. For a minority of migrants, the costs of migration were sizable, owing to long periods of initial unemployment, excessive job turnover, or other failures to adjust to the urban way of life. For the majority, however, because they had information about the city before coming and because their experiences after arrival were not too arduous, the costs of migration were low.

The second conclusion suggested by this chapter concerns the nature of urban problems and their relation to commitment. Apparently no special problems were faced by the migrants. Of course, the predominantly urban origin of the migrants to Santiago obviated the most pressing problems which rural-urban migration, by contrast, would engender. No evidence from the interviews with social workers suggested any difference in degree of commitment between migrants and natives.

These conclusions, in turn, lead to a further observation. A lack of outstanding urban adjustment problems for the migrants means that they function as producers of goods or services more swiftly and continuously after their arrival in Santiago than if they had been troubled by a series of adjustment difficulties. Within the microcosm that Santiago represents, the observed migration has been more efficient as an allocator of labor resources than a more primitive rural-urban migration would have been.

[15] Unfortunately, birthplace was not among the data collected.

8

Findings and Conclusions

Review of Findings

This book was introduced by a quotation from Professor Ranis that mentioned the necessity during economic development for a shift from agricultural to nonagricultural employment. To begin, we tried to ascertain the relative rates of progress of the agricultural and manufacturing sectors of the Chilean economy, beset, as they were, by problems of population growth, inflation, and an increasingly unequal distribution of income. In contrast with the decade of the 1940's, a decline in per capita real incomes resulted from these difficulties during the 1950's. The relative industrial distribution of the labor force compares the speed of the transition between agriculture and the rest of the economy during the two decades. The static character of the labor force distribution during the 1950's is apparent from the following table:

	Industrial Distribution of the Labor Force		
	1940	1952	1960
Agriculture	38.5%	29.7%	27.5%
Mining	4.4	4.8	4.1
Secondary sector	21.9	23.9	24.2
Tertiary sector	28.4	38.0	38.8
Unidentified	6.8	3.6	5.4
Total	100.0%	100.0%	100.0%

It might be helpful to review some of the findings of the body of the work in the light of the diverse theoretical viewpoints suggested in the second chapter. The costs-and-returns model of Schultz and

101

Sjaastad was never contradicted by the empirically derived data. Costs of migration were somewhat lower than might have been anticipated. Returns could be correspondingly low without diminishing the rate of return from investment in migration and, hence, without lowering the rate at which migration was occurring. This, in fact, seems to have been the case: as we saw, fully half of Santiago's labor force was born elsewhere in Chile or abroad.

The Ravenstein-Redford pattern of stage-like migratory movement was convincingly replicated by the Chilean experience. These patterns, found first in the England of the Industrial Revolution, were also present in Chile, despite the differences in the economic and other circumstances surrounding the movement. Rural-urban migration, at least to the biggest city, was a less important factor within the Chilean internal migration than was interurban movement. Many of the other features characteristic of the Chilean migrants seem plausible, if not obvious, when the interurban character of the migration is accepted.

Finally, we turn to those interactions between economic growth and internal migration suggested by Kuznets and others. Here the picture is considerably less clear, for a number of reasons. The foremost problem was a common one for development economists — lack of comparable regional wage data by which to measure, however roughly, the income alternatives facing potential migrants. This gap in the desirable data is one of the first which should be filled by any further research in this area.

The selectivity of the migration process was once again demonstrated; as in other countries, internal migrants in Chile stood at the beginning of their lifetimes of work. This youthfulness was coupled with educational and occupational attributes that indicated the capability of the urban migrants to compete with the people whom they joined in the city.

Conclusions

Before undertaking this study, we might have hypothesized that the growth of Santiago had been largely the result of migration from the rural areas of Chile, with all the social disorganization generally thought to accompany rural-urban migration. Considering Chile as an underdeveloped country, we might also have thought that one of the clearest imperatives for development would be a shift off the farms and into urban industry.

The findings of the investigation, presented in the preceding chapters, have served to modify both these *a priori* impressions. In the first place, the rural sector, which is to say the agricultural sector of the Chilean economy, has already shrunk considerably. In the least developed countries, it is not unusual to find 60% or even 70% of the occupied population engaged in agriculture. In Chile, on the other hand, as early as 1907, census data reveal that fewer than 40% of the labor force worked in agriculture. By 1960, the proportion had declined to 27.5%. At the same time, domestic income generated in agricultural pursuits was considerably below the average for nonagricultural occupations: the population working in agriculture in 1960 managed to produce only 12.2% of the domestic income in that year.

Second, even while realizing the magnitude of the relative rural-agricultural shrinkage within the Chilean economy, the predominantly urban origin of the Santiago migrants was surprising. A far greater proportion came to Santiago from other cities than would be expected if the migrants were drawn randomly from the population outside Santiago. Rural-urban migration was only a miniscule fraction of the total movement toward Santiago. In addition, our previous examination of rural-urban birth rate differentials and growth rates of cities of varying sizes leads to the conclusion that the emigrants from rural areas were settling in the cities of fewer than 50,000 people. This, in turn, suggests a two-generation model of migration: a first-generation migration from the rural areas to the towns and a second-generation movement to the capital city.

Meanwhile, the change in the structure of the economy has been painfully slow. Desirable, of course, would be a much swifter rise in agricultural production and productivity and a greater shift in the existing urban labor force from service and commercial activities into modern industrial ones. It might be said that the migration to the Chilean urban areas, which has left only one-third of the population in rural areas according to the census classification, has set the stage for further industrialization. The abrupt changes usually associated with the shift from a rural environment to an urban one have already been experienced. The task for the economy now is the creation of employment opportunities in modern industrial plants within existing urban centers — plants that would more effectively use the labor resources already located in these centers. That the migrants are no less employable than the natives is shown from their educational attainments and present occupational and industrial distributions.

Chilean policy makers face a number of alternatives that would affect future migration. The continuation of present government policies would mean the continuation of the type of migration experienced in the past. On the other hand, this interurban migration can either be accelerated or retarded by a number of measures.

Differences in land tenure arrangements, for instance, would affect the nature of the migration. More rapid rural emigration into the small towns would be furthered by a land reform which concentrated on large-scale holdings of the corporate agricultural type. In contrast, a land reform emphasizing family-sized farms (as the current land reform plans do) and the maintenance of the present agricultural population on the land would retard this rural emigration.

Educational policy decisions clearly affect the nature of the migration. If education trains young people for opportunities not available in the area, further migration will be stimulated. On the other hand, vocational education emphasizing, say, farm skills in the rural areas and the processing of agricultural and forest products in the small towns would have the opposite effect.

Although the elasticity of movement in response to the creation of infrastructure capital is uncertain, it was clear that public housing programs were more concentrated in the largest cities than in the outlying districts. It seems inescapable that this concentration would encourage further migration to these cities.

Fiscal policies could either alter or extend current trends in urban migration. Continuation of the *status quo* will result in the continued centralization of economic activity in Santiago. On the other hand, a conscious government attempt at industrial decentralization could offer tax incentives, the creation of industrial parks, and preferential freight rates to investors willing to engage in activity outside the capital. The Italian experience in the Mezzogiorno would be relevant to any industrial location policy decisions.

Finally, the requirement that most government spending and administrative decisions be centrally approved, usually at the ministerial level, will tend to continue the present centralization in government policy making.[1] A conscious decentralization policy would emphasize local control of spending where knowledge of local conditions was likely to be more timely than or superior to knowledge in the capital.

---

[1] According to an official publication, the Minister of Education himself has to sign 300 documents a day. See Ministerio de Educación Pública, *Bases generales para el planeamiento de la educación chilena* (Santiago, 1961), p. 48.

None of these decisions can be made overnight. Nevertheless if the problems raised by the persistent Chilean migration are going to be solved, and if the potentials for economic development inherent in the migration are going to be tapped, then policy makers will have to face the need for making such decisions.

Appendices

Appendix A

The Santiago Labor Force Survey of the University of Chile's Institute of Economics

Many of the findings in the thesis rely on results drawn from published and unpublished data of the labor force survey of the University of Chile's Institute of Economics. Within Greater Santiago, the survey has been conducted since 1956. Other cities and some rural areas have also been surveyed, especially since 1960. In all, twenty surveys were made in Greater Santiago between October 1956 and September 1963. Other areas and the number of surveys in each were Valparaíso–Viña del Mar — 10, Concepción — 14, Valdivia — 5, La Serena-Coquimbo — 6, Antofagasta — 6, Iquique — 5, Puerto Montt — 4, O'Higgins province — 1, and a five-province region around Concepción — 1.

The data usually requested of each person surveyed included:

1. Relationship with the head of the household.
2. Sex.
3. Age.
4. Whether employed, seeking work, or outside the labor force.
5. Occupation.
6. Whether employer, white-collar worker, blue-collar worker, own-account worker, unpaid family worker, or domestic servant.
7. Industry group in which employed.
8. Number of hours worked during the past week.
9. If unemployed or seasonally inactive, duration of unemployment or seasonal inactivity.

In addition, in some of the surveys, other characteristics such as income, education, place of birth, length of residence, and participation in trade union activity were explored. As noted in the text and tables of the

109

book, the data on place of birth and length of residence within Greater Santiago were extensively used, together with the data on age, sex, unemployment, occupation, industrial distribution, and education.

The Institute's sample in Greater Santiago was a randomly selected one of households.[1] The area of Greater Santiago was defined to contain eleven *comunas*: Santiago, Providencia, San Miguel, Quinta Normal, Conchalí, Ñuñoa, Renca, Barrancas, Cisterna, La Granja, and Las Condes. For practical purposes, the survey's definition of Greater Santiago and that of the census are the same.[2]

The random sample was chosen after dividing the area into its census zones. Thirty-two geographic strata were determined which were, within themselves, approximately homogeneous with respect to income levels. These strata, in turn, were divided into subunits, each with about forty families. Finally about three hundred of these subunits were chosen at random. A careful census of the addresses and families within these subunits was conducted. From within these enumerated families, one-fifth were finally chosen at random to be surveyed. The size of the sample was thus about 12,000 people and held about 4,500 labor force members. At the same time, estimates of total Santiago population and labor force were 2,196,500 and 778,300 respectively, in June 1963.

Unemployment, the principal measurement goal of the survey, was thought to fall within a range of from 5% to 7% of the labor force. Given this range, the sample size meant that the probability was 0.95 that the unemployment rate would be within 12% of true unemployment. Owing to the nature of the binomial distribution, higher unemployment (more than 7%) could be determined more accurately with the same sample size; lower unemployment (less than 5%) with somewhat less accuracy.

[1] The following description of the selection of the Greater Santiago sample draws heavily on Carlos Clavel G., "Estudios de mano de obra y desocupación en zonas urbanas y en la provincia de O'Higgins — análisis metodológico" (Santiago: University of Chile, unpublished commercial engineering thesis, 1962).

[2] For the exact census definition of the "ciudad de Santiago," see *XII censo general de población* (Santiago: Servicio Nacional de Estadística y Censos, 1956), III, xi.

Appendix B

Sample Survey of
Recent Migrants

In order to determine certain migrant characteristics more directly than
had been done in the past, a survey was conducted of migrants with the
following characteristics:

1. Active in the labor force.
2. Length of residence of less than ten years (i.e., nine or fewer years).
3. Not working as a live-in domestic servant (*empleada doméstica
   puertas adentro*).

In this survey we wanted to talk about their migration experiences with
labor force members rather than with housewives, students, and others
inactive in the labor force. Secondly, the fraction of migrants with more
than ten years of residence in Santiago, as noted in the thesis, was large.
Many of the adjustment and employment problems of these migrants
would have already been solved. In addition, it was felt that more recent
migrants would give more accurate responses, since the time lag between
migration and our interviews was shorter than it would have been for
those with ten or more years of residence. Finally, we decided not to talk
with live-in domestic servants. The occupations of these people, for the
most part women, are not central to the development process. Furthermore, it would have been difficult to obtain candid answers from them,
since most of the interviews would, of necessity, have been conducted in
the presence of their employers.

Given these qualifications for inclusion in the survey, we noted the
address of any migrant with these characteristics who was surveyed in
the Greater Santiago labor force sample survey (described in Appendix
A) in June 1963. These data were drawn from the original completed
questionnaires of that survey.

The questionnaire used appears on the following pages. It was formulated with the help of members of the Institute's employment survey

111

section on the basis of their survey experience. Some of the words used were *chilenismos* (Chilean idioms) rather than academic Spanish. These words were chosen for their ease of recognition among the people to be surveyed. In addition, a small pilot survey or pretest was conducted prior to the survey itself, and the questionnaire was modified on the basis of experience thus gained.

The interviews were made during January 1964. The interviewing was done by a fifth-year student in economics from the University of Chile. He was chosen on the basis of his extensive experience as an interviewer (*encuestador*) and group leader with the larger Institute employment survey. Three hundred and ten usable responses resulted from this interview process, and these form the basis for the conclusions drawn from the survey.

RESULTS OF THE SURVEY OF ECONOMICALLY ACTIVE RECENT MIGRANTS, JANUARY 1964

	Classification Immediately Upon Arrival		
	Economically Active	Economically Inactive	All
Lived only one place before			
first coming to Santiago	60.6%	73.2%	62.9%
Two places	23.6	8.9	21.0
Three places	7.5	12.5	8.4
Four or more places	8.3	5.4	7.7
Lived in Santiago for one			
continuous extended period	87.8%	92.9%	88.7%
More than one period of residence			
in Santiago	12.2	7.1	11.3
Size of birthplace in 1960:			
Less than 1,000 inhabitants	16.1%	8.9%	14.8%
1,000–5,000	10.2	10.7	10.3
5,000–10,000	7.1	16.1	8.7
10,000–20,000	15.0	10.7	14.2
20,000–50,000	16.5	16.1	16.5
50,000–100,000	18.5	26.8	20.0
more than 100,000	9.1	10.7	9.4
born outside Chile	7.5	—	6.1
First occupation in Santiago:			
Professionals and technicians	11.0%	25.0%	13.5%
Managers and administrators	2.4	—	1.9
Owners	5.5	1.8	4.8
Office workers	15.0	14.3	14.8
Salesmen	7.1	8.9	7.4
Farmers	1.2	—	1.0
Miners	0.4	—	0.3
Drivers	2.8	—	2.3
Artisans and operatives	25.2	7.1	21.9
Manual and unskilled workers	14.2	7.1	12.9
Service workers	15.4	8.9	14.2
No data	—	26.8	4.8
Active or not active upon			
arrival	81.9%	18.1%	100.0%

SURVEY OF RECENT MIGRANTS (*Continued*)

	Percentage of Respondents
Delay in finding work for those economically active immediately upon arrival:	
No delay	40.6%
1 week	6.7
2 weeks	5.5
3–4 weeks	9.8
2–3 months	10.2
4–6 months	7.9
7–12 months	8.7
2 years	3.1
more than 2 years	2.0
no data	5.5
Did the respondent engage in casual labor before finding a steady job?	
Yes	7.1%
No	73.6%
No data	19.3
Number of jobs held during first year of residence in Santiago:	
(unemployed during first year)	11.4%
1	73.6
2	11.0
3	2.8
4 or more	1.2
Did the respondent ever come to Santiago before coming to live?	
Yes	54.5%
No	44.2
No data	1.3
Before coming to live in Santiago, did the respondent have friends or relatives living in Santiago?	
Yes	83.9%
No	14.5
No data	1.6
When the respondent came to Santiago to live, did he bring:	
His whole family?	40.3%
Part of it?	9.7
Was he alone?	48.7
No data	1.3

SURVEY OF RECENT MIGRANTS (*Continued*)

	Percentage of Respondents
By what means of transportation did the respondent come to Santiago?	
Train	62.3%
Auto	1.9
Bus	15.8
Truck	5.5
Plane	4.2
Ship	5.8
No data	4.5
Intentions for the future:	
To remain in Santiago	79.0%
To return to the place of origin	5.2
To move to some other place	4.5
"Depends" on the job opportunities	6.1
Already returned to place of origin	2.3
No data	2.9
Knowledge of others who have returned:	
Yes	14.5%
No	39.4
Not sure	25.2
No data	21.0

INSTITUTO DE ECONOMÍA — UNIVERSIDAD DE CHILE
ENCUESTA SOBRE MIGRACIÓN

Estrato_____Segmento_____Dirección_____

	Edad cuando se fue	Tiempo de residencia

1. Lugar de nacimiento_____
   Otors lugares_____

2. Después de llegar a Santiago, cuál fue su primer trabajo estable? . . . .
   Si fuera estudiante o inactivo en la fuerza de trabajo, haga una cruz en "estudiante" o "inactivo" . . . .
   Para los activos: Cuánto tiempo se demoró en encontrarlo? . . . .
   Tuvo pololos antes de encontrar este primer trabajo estable? . . . .
   Si es así, cuánto tiempo se demoró en encontrarlo? . . . .

2. Oficio:
   _____

   Estudiante_____
   Inactivo_____

   _____

   Sí_____No_____

   _____

3. Para los activos durante el primer año en Santiago:
   Para cuántos establecimientos, empresas (etc.) distintas trabajó ud. durante su primer año acá? . . . .
   Para los trabajadores por cuenta propia o empleadores: cuántas ocupaciones distintas tuvo durante su primer año acá? . .

3.

   _____

   _____

4. Viajó Ud. a Santiago antes de trasladarse acá? Vivían algunos amigos o parientes acá a los cuales conocía antes de venir? . . . .

4. Sí_____No_____

   Sí_____No_____

5. Cuando vino Ud. a Santiago a buscar trabajo por primera vez (o a establecerse), le acompañó a Ud. . . . .
   Por qué vía llegó a Santiago? . . . .

5. Su esposa e hijos?_____
   Algun otro pariente?_____
   O era solo?_____
   Tren_____Auto_____Bus_____
   Camión_____Avión_____
   Otro (especificar)_____

6. Piensa Ud. quedarse acá en Santiago permanentemente o tiene planes de volver a . . . (su lugar de origen)? O a algun otro lugar? . . . .

6. Quiere quedarse acá._____
   Quiere volver a_____
   Quiere ubicarse en otro lugar. (dónde?)_____

7. Conoce a alguien de . . . (su lugar) que haya venido a Santiago a trabajar y se haya devuelto a . . . (su lugar de origen)? Si es así, anote las razones de hacerlo en el otro lado de esta hoja. . . .

7.

   Sí_____No_____

Bibliographic Note

This note mentions works about the Chilean economy which bear on the issues discussed in this book. The citations in the footnotes to the text deal with these issues in a more general fashion. As a result they are not all repeated here. On the other hand, the state of most North American library collections of material on Chile can only be described as deplorable. Accordingly and somewhat frustratingly, research sometimes seems possible only on the spot.

The most readily available over-all survey of Chile's geography is Preston James's textbook, *Latin America* (New York, 1959), Chapter 7. Another general and readable treatment is Gilbert Butland, *Chile* (London, 1956). Economic geography has been covered in the four-volume work by the Corporación de Fomento (CORFO), *Geografía económica de Chile* (Santiago, 1950 and 1962).

Empirical data on the Chilean economy arise from a number of diverse sources. The government's Dirección de Estadística y Censos issues a monthly bulletin, *Estadística chilena,* with annual resumés. Publication of these resumés frequently falls two or three years late, and no official preliminary estimates fill this gap. The other very general and very standard source of economic statistics is the Banco Central's *Boletín mensual,* which covers many fields in addition to the expected monetary and commercial ones.

National accounts statistics are compiled by CORFO; the most recent set at the time of this writing seems to be *Cuentas nacionales de Chile 1940–1962 (cifas provisionales revisadas);* (Santiago, 1963; mimeographed). The most recently published official data cover only the years 1940–1954, and these numbers have been subsequently unofficially revised. CORFO is also the source of Chile's national plan, *Programa nacional de desarrollo económico 1961–1970* (Santiago, n.d.). CORFO's own activities during its early years have been described by Herman Finer for the ILO in *The Chilean Development Corporation — A Study in National Planning To Raise Living Standards* (Montreal, 1947). More recent treatments include those by CORFO itself, *Veinte años de labor 1939–1959* and the annual *Memoria.*

The University of Chile's Institute of Economics has systematized and commented on Chilean economic trends since 1940 in two of its most successful publications, *Desarrollo económico de Chile 1940–1956* and

117

La economía de Chile en el período 1950–1963 (two volumes). A United States Department of Commerce book that sets itself much the same global task is the informative *Investment in Chile — Basic Information for U.S. Businessmen* by Merwin L. Bohan and Morton Pomeranz (Washington, D.C., 1960). One monthly magazine deals with general economic subjects, *Panorama económico*. The more scholarly reviews include *Economía*, published by the Faculty of Economic Sciences of the (National) University of Chile, and *Cuadernos de economía*, published by the same faculty in the Catholic University of Chile. Two books on the economic aspects of Chilean history, written within the context of the inflation and stagnation of the 1950's, are Aníbal Pinto's *Chile — Un caso de desarrollo frustrado* (Santiago, 1962) and Jorge Ahumada's *En vez de la miseria* (Santiago, 1960). North American economists may find themselves more attracted by Markos Mamalakis and Clark Reynolds, *Essays on the Chilean Economy* (Homewood, Illinois: Irwin, 1965).

The Chilean inflation has been the subject of a great deal of research, both in this country and in Chile. The best analytical articles are those cited in Chapter 1. In addition, Nicholas Kaldor's view, representing a "structuralist" approach, should be mentioned, "Problemas económicos de Chile," *Trimestre Económico* (Mexico), Vol. 26, No. 2 (April-June 1959), 170–221.

Regional aspects of economic activity, as lamented earlier, are almost completely ignored in statistical compilations. CORFO wrote about its "Comites provinciales de desarrollo" with the optimistic subtitle "Un mecanismo dinámico para el desarrollo económico" in *Panorama económico*, No. 232 (July 1962). Alvaro Marfan also discussed some of these regional issues in an address entitled "Desarrollo y fomento regionales," reprinted in *Industria* (Santiago), No. 70 (September 1960). Robert T. Brown and Carlos Hurtado have treated Chile's transportation problems in *Una política de transportes para Chile* (Santiago: Institute of Economics, 1963). But the best data sources which classify activities regionally are still the population, manufacturing, and agricultural censuses of the Dirección de Estadística y Censos.

Bibliographically the most discouraging aspect of economic research in Chile is the existence of government documents which are not circulated to any libraries, domestic or foreign. The annual *memorias* and budgets of the government's ministries are but one example. Frequently these reports contain a wealth of detailed information about the activities of the ministry and about the sector which it is supposed to serve, but these reports, although published, are not circulated systematically and can only be discovered by personal visits and contacts.

Population and its composition is covered most thoroughly in the population census, the twelfth of which was carried out in 1952, appearing in five volumes in 1956. The 1960 census had not been published at the time this research was carried out. Preliminary results, from a sample of the census, had appeared in a number of short pamphlets, *Algunos resultados del XIII censo de población y II de vivienda obtenidos por muestreo, Algunos resultados provinciales del II censo de vivienda obtenidos por muestreo, Cifras comparativas de los censos de 1940 y 1952 y muestra del censo de 1960*, and *Cifras provisorias del número de habitantes y de viviendas según censo de población de 1960*. The Dirección de Estadística y Censos also issues an annual volume, *Demografía* and an even less regular *Boletín de estadísticas demográficas*.

The UN's Economic Commission for Latin America has been instrumental in making still further estimates of demographic variables for Chile. Its most recent efforts, which treat the whole of Latin America, appear in two articles in the *Economic Bulletin for Latin America*: "The Demographic Situation in Latin America" (Vol. 6, No. 2, October 1961, 13–52) and "Geographic Distribution of the Population of Latin America and Regional Development Priorities" (Vol. 8, No. 1, March 1963, 51–63).

The best, in fact the only, employment data for the nation as a whole come from the population census. In the biggest cities, the Institute of Economics has carried out sample surveys of employment, much like those of the U.S. The results have been published since 1956, and on a quarterly basis since 1960, under the title *Ocupación y desocupación*. Early surveys of Santiago are reported in the Institute's *Población del Gran Santiago* (1957). Other Institute publications centered on labor force issues include Rudolf C. Blitz's *Algunas características de edad, educación e ingreso de la fuerza de trabajo* (1962), and *Movilidad de la mano de obra* (1960). Carlos Clavel's unpublished thesis for the Faculty of Economic Sciences of the University of Chile, "Estudios de mano de obra y desocupación en zonas urbanas y en la provincia de O'Higgins — Análisis metodológico" (1962) deals with some of the more technical statistical points surrounding this particular sample survey.

Education in general and human capital in particular are treated in the Instituto de Organización y Administración, *Estudio de recursos humanos de nivel universitario en Chile* (Santiago, 1962). More generally, Eduardo Hamuy has addressed himself to educational problems in *Educación elemental, analfabetismo y desarrollo económico* (Santiago, 1960) and, with others, *El problema educacional del pueblo chileno* (Santiago, 1961). The Ministry of Public Education expounded its educational philosophy in *Bases generales para el planeamiento de la educación chilena* (1961). The University of Chile's Instituto de Educacción has issued a yearbook, *Año pedagógico*, since 1959.

Finally, the first systematic empirical work on Chilean internal migration was done by the Institute of Economics. Their *Población del Gran Santiago*, already mentioned, examines the problem. An unpublished thesis for the Faculty of Economics of the University of Chile by Ivan Yáñez, "Características principales de la migración hacia el Gran

Santiago" (1958) deals with much the same material. The Institute's 1959 publication *La migración interna en Chile en el período 1940–1952* calculates the extent of the intercensal net migration by *departamentos*. Carlos Munizaga discusses some of the anthropological implications of one of the migrant streams in his *Estructuras transicionales en la migración de los araucanos de hoy a la ciudad de Santiago de Chile* (Universidad de Chile, Notas del Centro de Estudios Antropológicos, No. 6, 1961).

In April 1962, the Centro Latinoamericano de Demografía (CELADE) carried out a massive sample survey of Santiago migrants, the results of which have not been completely published. Preliminary findings appear in a series of mimeographed bulletins entitled "Encuesta sobre la migración en el Gran Santiago." More generally, some of the essays in the UNESCO book *Urbanization in Latin America* (Paris, 1961) dealt with diverse aspects of the urban migration in some of the other Latin American countries.

Readers who wish to pursue bibliographic inquiries further are referred to the bibliography in my M.I.T. doctoral dissertation for the Department of Economics, "Internal Migration, Unemployment, and Economic Growth in Postwar Chile" (June 1964).

Index

Index